Reminiscences of Caroline Austen

Reminiscences of
CAROLINE AUSTEN

Introduction by Deirdre Le Faye

The Jane Austen Society

First published in Great Britain in 1986
by The Jane Austen Society

Copyright © 1986 Mr and Mrs Lawrence Impey
Introduction and Notes Copyright © 1986
Deirdre Le Faye

ISBN 0 951103 5 0 4

Typeset by TJB Photosetting Ltd, South Witham, Lincolnshire
Printed in Great Britain by Biddles Ltd, Guildford

Contents

Illustrations

Maps

Acknowledgments

The illustrations are reproduced by kind permission:
1 Joan Austen-Leigh; 2 Mrs T.M. Morrish; 4 Mike
Edwards. 3 and 6 were photographed by Brian
McGlashan. The two maps are reproduced from the
Ordnance Survey 1″ first edition.

Introduction

Caroline Mary Craven Austen (1805–80), the writer of these reminiscences, was Jane Austen's niece, the second daughter of Jane's eldest brother James. As Caroline relates, her father's first wife Anne Mathew had died young, and she was the child of his second marriage, to Mary Lloyd. From her birth in 1805 until her father's death in 1819 Caroline lived in the rectory at Steventon, where James had succeeded his father George Austen as incumbent. During these first years of her life she and her parents were in close contact with all the residents of Steventon whom Jane Austen herself had known as neighbours until her removal to Bath in 1801. Furthermore, as the Lloyds had been friends of the Austens since the 1780s, a friendship culminating in the marriage of Mary to James in 1797, all the Craven family history which Mary retailed to Caroline would have been well known also to Jane. Caroline's reminiscences, although they do not make many specific references to her aunt, illuminate the background against which the latter lived and wrote, and provide further information on the people and events mentioned in Jane's correspondence.

Caroline's own life was singularly quiet and uneventful. Her brother James-Edward and her half-sister Anna were respectively seven and twelve years her senior. As a consequence her childhood seems to have been fairly solitary. When she visited Chawton there were Austen cousins near her own age to play with, but her Fowle cousins at Kintbury were all older and she apparently had no contemporary companions at Steventon. An early sketch shows her as a pretty little girl with dark curly hair; when she was fourteen her father told his aunt, Mrs Leigh Perrot: 'Caroline has that playfulness of mind united with an affectionate heart, which so peculiarly marked our lamented Jane'.[1] Like her brother and half-sister, in her childhood Caroline wrote stories which were proudly sent to her Aunt Jane for comment –

1

although one at least was not a success, as family tradition recalled:

> Caroline believed it to be a necessary part of a tragedy that all the *dramatis personae* should somehow meet their end, by violence or otherwise, in the last act; and this belief produced such a scene of carnage and woe as to cause fits of laughter among unsympathetic elders, and tears to the author, who threw the unfortunate tragedy into the fire on the spot.[2]

The 'unsympathetic elders' here presumably did not include Jane, for Caroline remembered how patiently and kindly her aunt had received these youthful efforts, always finding some praise to bestow. But Jane eventually recommended her niece to pay more attention to solid learning rather than scribbling stories, and Caroline dutifully obeyed this suggestion. Towards the end of her life, indeed, she came to look back in prim Victorian disapproval upon her childish essays, and a few years before her death destroyed what remained of them.

Following James Austen's death in 1819 his widow Mary (Lloyd) and her two children moved to Berkshire, where they lived together for some years in a variety of rented houses in the Newbury district, while James-Edward finished his Oxford studies, took Holy Orders, and entered upon his first curacy at Newtown on the outskirts of Newbury. In 1828 James-Edward married Emma Smith and joined her family at Tring for the first few years of their wedded life. At this time Emma described Caroline as being 'a very sweet sensible girl, and Mamma and we all like her exceedingly'.[3] But despite these attractive qualities there is not the slightest hint of any romance entering into her life, nor is any man's name ever linked with hers. She continued to live with her mother until Mary's death in 1843, whiling away her time by such tasks as making for her brother 'a large arm-chair, of which the back, seat, and arms were covered with roses in various tints on a black ground, the flowers and the background being worked by herself, in coloured wools on canvas, the whole being executed in cross-stitch.'[4]

2

After her mother's death Caroline moved to Wargrave in order to be near her brother's home Scarlets, at Hare Hatch. From then on she devoted her life to being a good aunt to Anna's seven children, and James-Edward's nine surviving out of ten. As her niece Mary-Augusta Austen-Leigh remembered:

> All the nephews and nieces, as they grew older, found her not less agreeable as a companion than she was kind as an aunt. She joined an excellent memory, and an original and cultivated mind, to a sweet, gentle manner, and, having gifts both of humour and pathos, she could make everything she related interesting or amusing to her hearers. These powers, and the unselfishness of her nature, made her greatly beloved, and a most welcome guest, not only to us and to all her own relations, but to all our mother's sisters, and to their husbands also, when they could persuade her to pay them a visit.[5]

However, in middle life Caroline became partially deaf and suffered from tinnitus, which to some extent made her withdraw from society. For the last twenty years of her life she lived at Frog Firle, near Alfriston, Sussex, where she kept house for her nephews Charles and Spencer Austen-Leigh, two of James-Edward's sons who had remained bachelors.

In the early 1860s James-Edward planned to write a biography of Jane Austen, and asked his two sisters to help in this work. Caroline wrote out her memories of their aunt in 1867, and some of this information was used by her brother in his *Memoir of Jane Austen* published in 1869.[6] The interest of recalling the past evidently encouraged Caroline to write her own reminiscences, and at some time, presumably in the early 1870s, she began the manuscript which now follows. By 20th July 1873 she had completed her retrospect up to the beginning of the year 1820. After that date, she realised it would be too difficult to attempt to record a complete history of a large and increasing family group, so she contented herself by noting down what seemed to her personally significant dates and events. However, as so very little happened during her long spinsterhood, entries after 1820 become increasingly trivial and inconsequent; in this

3

edited version, therefore, only those which have bearing on the Austen family descent or are of general historical interest have been included.

Two versions of the manuscript exist, divided unequally between four soft-covered quarto notebooks. Each version contains some information not given in the other, and both have marginal additions, cancellations, some pages cut out and others roughly pasted in; it is not possible to decide which, if either, was intended to be the final text. This published text is a collation which aims to give the maximum relevant information. Explanatory notes and comments are added at the end of Caroline's work. At the time of writing there were some facts that Caroline did not know or could not remember, and at these points she leaves blank spaces in her manuscript; also occasionally in the flow of composition she omits a word. The correct facts or missing words are now inserted within square brackets [ ], as also are modern place-names where Caroline gives older or local versions. The punctuation has been to some extent modernised, and a few paragraphs have been rearranged to provide a more logical narrative. Opening sentences in quotation marks '' are those taken by Caroline direct from her mother's diaries as a starting-point from which to expand her own recollections.

DEIRDRE LE FAYE

REMINISCENCES OF CAROLINE AUSTEN

With abundant leisure, and with a natural inclination for looking backwards on what lies behind me, I desire to relate to myself, in correct succession, the events of my past life. Still, as plainly as ever, do I see the places where I once dwelt and the people amongst whom I lived. Still constantly am I companied by the shadows of the family to which I belonged – and words spoken, some of them trivial enough, and little incidents of no significance in their consequences, are yet perpetually rising up in my recollection – therefore thus far I see no danger of absolute forgetfulness. But my memory was never much guided by dates, and now I find I want them, and probably I shall want them yet more, to give clearness and truth to my recollections.

I do not intend to write my own life, or to record my own thoughts, nor do I intend to make much observation, for good or for bad, on what I recall; only, with the help of old pocket-books, to preserve the dates of various family events – deaths, marriages, removals and the like – some of which had their day of deep interest, and I cannot bear to think how all is passing into oblivion! Let *me* at least remember whilst I can!

The entries in my mother's well-kept pocket-books are the authorities, on which I write of these events, and give their dates. The enlargements which I may make on some of them, are from what she told me in after years, on several points of interest to us. The dates of each year I shall give from her diaries, relating what I have further to say, in my own words – as indeed I must do, for she scarcely ever added any remark to the fact which she wrote down. Many particulars did I also hear from herself of her own early days. They were always very interesting to me, and as she was the first who gave me any histories of the past, to which when quite a child I was delighted to listen, it comes most naturally to me now, to begin my recollections with her family. For my first date I open the pocket-book of the year

1804

In June died my great-uncle, Mr John Craven, quite suddenly I believe, of apoplexy, at Chilton House, near Hungerford. A stroke of the same nature had previously fallen on my grandmother Mrs Lloyd, his sister. To her it did not prove fatal, but it impaired her mind and memory, as well as her health. Fearful that the shock of such bad tidings might bring on a second attack, her daughters decided on not telling her, and they refrained from wearing their mourning in her presence. But one day she astonished [them] by saying suddenly, 'Why does not the bell go for my brother?' – and from that moment she accepted the fact of his death. Whether her wandering imagination had presented to her this idea, or whether she had heard some servants' talk, they never knew; but they no longer concealed the fact, and she acquiesced in it very tranquilly.[7]

December 16th 'Died Mrs Lefroy of Ashe.' On the 21st my father buried her. She was greatly lamented and her end was a sad one. She was riding a very quiet horse, attended by a servant, as usual. My father saw her in Overton, and she observed the animal she rode was so stupid and lazy, she could scarcely make him canter. My father rode homeward, she staying to do some errands in Overton; next morning the news of her death reached Steventon. After getting to the top of Overton Hill, the horse seemed to be running away – it was not known whether anything had frightened him – the servant, unwisely, rode up to catch the bridle rein – missed his hold and the animal darted off faster. He could not give any clear account, but it was supposed that Mrs Lefroy in her terror, threw herself off, and fell heavily on the hard ground. She never spoke afterwards, and she died in a few hours. She was a woman most highly gifted, and had the power of attaching and influencing all who came near her in an unusual manner. She had the happiest manners, and they truly expressed the benevolence of her heart. Such was the record that remained of her, in my early days, amongst her

6

old neighbours, and I learnt to think of her as having been a perfect model of gracefulness and goodness. She was sister to Sir Egerton Brydges of Kent.[8]

1805

On January 21st died my grandfather, the Revd George Austen, quite suddenly also, at Bath, aged [73].

At Ibthorp died, April 16th, my grandmother Mrs Lloyd, who from repeated paralytic seizures had been failing in mind and body for some time past. She was buried at Up Hurstbourne [Hurstbourne Tarrant]. She was [76] years of age.

My mother had been married from Ibthorp, leaving only one sister, Martha, at home. The other sister, Eliza, had married, many years before, from Enborne, her cousin the Revd Fulwar Craven Fowle.

With Mrs Lloyd had also lived to the last Mrs Stent, an early friend, of rather inferior position in life, and reduced, from family misfortunes, to very narrow means. I remember her quite an old lady, lodging at Highclere in a small cottage, near to Mrs Criswick.[9]

Mrs Lloyd was a daughter of the Honble Charles Craven, Governor of South Carolina in the reign of [Queen Anne].[10] He married Elizabeth, daughter of the Honble Col John Staples. In the early part of their married life they lived at Lenchwick in Worcestershire – the place was left to him by a brother – and there most of their children were born. Then they lived at Sennington [Sevenhampton] in Gloucestershire, and at last at Brimpton, near Newbury, where he died. They had a family of three sons and five daughters; only one *son,* John, lived to grow up. Of the five daughters the eldest was Mrs Cox, married early in life to a Squire Cox, of good degree. A suitable marriage, but I do not know much about him. Then there was Mrs Fowle, Mrs Lloyd, Mrs Hinxman and Mrs Bishop – but I may not have named them in their right order, as to age.

My grandmother, Martha Craven, and her sisters, had but a rough life of it. Their mother, a most courteous and fascinating woman in society, was of a stern tyrannical temper,

7

and they were brought up in *fear*, not in *love*. They were sometimes not allowed proper food, but were required to eat what was loathsome to them, and were often relieved from hunger by the maids privately bringing them up bread and cheese after they were in bed. Perhaps some of the traditions of Mrs Craven's personal cruelty to her children, as endangering even their lives, went beyond the truth, but there could be no doubt that she was a very unkind and severe mother. I do not hear that their father ever interfered – the family seemed to be left to her. I suppose he was very much away from home.

It was from Sennington that my grandmother's adventures began. She and her other sisters, when young women, were left there for some months, whilst their mother was making visits in Berkshire, staying chiefly at Barton Court – Mr Raymond's. She was accustomed to take with her one daughter when she went from home – to wait upon her, as was said – and at the time to which I refer, she had taken Jane, afterwards Mrs Fowle. At Sennington there lived a family named Hinxman, not in the ranks of gentility, well-to-do yeomen farming their own small property. Mr Hinxman aspired to the hand of one of the Miss Cravens, and obtained it. They were married during her mother's absence in Berkshire; and still worse, a friend of his, Mr Bishop, a horse-dealer, as I have heard, with no money and no character, prevailed on another daughter, Mary, to marry him. Where Governor Craven was, all this time, I do not know; but apparently not with his wife, nor at home with his daughters.

The Hinxman marriage turned out not so very bad, but Mrs Bishop's was deplorable. She was left a destitute widow, with one daughter, Mary Bishop, much of an invalid, and was helped a little by her nieces. They lived on, both mother and daughter, at Fairford, in my recollection, though I never saw them.

My grandmother, Martha, knowing how much Mrs Craven would resent these misalliances, and foreseeing nothing but increased severity in the house, could not resolve to face her mother's anger, and *she* also left her home, before Mrs Craven could return to it, and she never lived under her parent's roof again.

All the sisters had had £500 apiece left them by their uncle, Lord Craven, and on the interest of this little portion she determined to try and live. She went to a Mrs Steel, who kept a girls' school at Tewkesbury. She paid her what she could for her board and made out the rest by helping sometimes in the school, and by doing plain needlework which she took in anonymously, for it was not to be known that Miss Craven was earning money as a sempstress. Mrs Steel had troubles of her own, and was herself very poor; but she was a good friend as far as she could be to her lodger, and she came once, long afterwards, to stay at Enborne, when my grandmother was in more prosperity.

These family histories were related to me without dates, and I cannot tell how long she stayed at Tewkesbury; but the next change that occurred was her leaving Tewkesbury and going to live with her brother and his wife, Mr and Mrs John Craven. *She* was a Miss Raymond of Barton (half-sister to Mr Jemmett Raymond the possessor of that place). She had a good fortune, with more in prospect; but she was a young woman of weak intellect, to whom some companion and guide was almost necessary. None could be found more fitting, than her husband's sister, and I was told that they agreed very well together; but the arrangement came to an end by Mr Craven's decree, much to the sorrow of his poor silly wife, who saw her sister-in-law replaced by a lady who was particularly obnoxious to her. She did not herself live very long.

My grandmother's next asylum was with her aunt, Mrs Willoughby, who lived in the Manor House of Bishopston, Wilts. There she became acquainted with Mr Lloyd, the vicar of the place, and she was married to him in Bishopston Church, 2nd June 1763. All their children – they had four – were born in Bishopston, but whilst their family was still very young, they removed to Enborne Rectory, near Newbury, Lord Craven, my grandmother's kinsman, giving Mr Lloyd that living. He retained Bishopston also.

The Revd Noyes Lloyd, my grandfather, was the son of

9

the Revd [John] Lloyd of Epping, Essex. *This* we only ascertained lately, for strange as it was, none of his grandchildren knew as much.

The Lloyds were supposed, of course, to have come originally from Wales, and it was assumed that their coat of arms, three wolves' heads, bore testimony to their country as plainly as their name. I never could learn *when* it was that they became English but for several generations the family had been settled in Norfolk. There was the estate, but the name of the place I cannot remember. With Mr Lloyd, the representative of the elder branch, my Aunt Martha kept up a cousinly correspondence to within my recollection, apprising each other of family events. They had known him a little in their younger days, and he had been with them at Enborne. I am sure the relationship was not *nearer* than second cousin. At last he died; and with *him* ended all thought of our Norfolk kindred.[11]

My grandfather, the Revd Noyes *or* Nowis Lloyd, was certainly the son of the Revd [John] Lloyd of Epping. There is in the Register the entry of his baptism, and of several other children. The mother's name was Isabella. I imagine *she* was an heiress of the name of Nowis or Noyes, for we have a coffee pot, on which the Nowis arms are quartered, as of an heiress, with those of Lloyd and Craven. I suppose the estate in Norfolk came by her, and descended to her eldest son, but it is surprising how little we ever knew about them, for a want of curiosity at the proper time for enquiry. The elder generation could have told us something distinct. My Aunt Martha was the last who had the clue to our family connections in that quarter. My grandfather's name seems to have been spelt indifferently Nowis or Noyes. He wrote it himself Nowis, in the Bishopston Registers; after he married, it was generally Noyes. I have heard too that it was my grandmother who changed the pronunciation of Lloyd into Floyd as it was always spoken in my recollection. They said *that* was the true Welsh pronunciation of double L, but a Welshman and a scholar has assured me it was useless to try and imitate their accent, the English tongue could not give it, and that we had therefore better say Lloyd.

10

Caroline as a child.
The drawing is unsigned, but the handwriting
is that of Cassandra Austen.

Memorial to Mr and Mrs Jemmett Raymond
in Kintbury Church.

I believe it was in 1771 that Mr and Mrs Lloyd took up their abode at Enborne. Four years afterwards the smallpox broke out in their family. All the children, and many of the servants, had it very badly. The son died; it was of the confluent sort, and those who recovered bore the marks of its virulence all through their lives. The few lines inscribed over the grave of the little boy, in Enborne churchyard, tell the short history of his life and death.

Charles Lloyd, only son of The Revd Noyes Lloyd, when 8 other persons in the same family recovered from the smallpox, died of that distemper on the 11th of April 1775 in the 7th year of his age.

The affliction of his death was long and deeply felt, as I have heard, by his parents; he was a very sweet-tempered child, and their fond recollections preserved all little traits of his childish goodness, and imagination concluded that, such as was the child, so would have been the man. In that dreadful malady, when all must have suffered so much from its fever and restlessness, they loved to remember how he thought of another rather than himself. His little sister, younger by two or three years, was fractious and trouble-some, and when she saw him put into the cot, she wanted to have it for herself; or if he lay in his mother's lap, she cried to be taken up instead; and he would say, 'Let sister have my place, Mama, for she is but a little thing'.

The smallpox was brought into the house by the coachman, who concealed the fact, till too late, that it was in his own cottage. My grandfather, when it broke out at the Rectory, separated himself from his family, and took lodgings – I *think* at Newtown – not to carry the infection into church on Sundays. The children had never been inoculated – I know not whether from any superstitious scruple on the part of their parents, or from a negligent delay.

The son was dead; but three daughters were left, to be educated, and grow up at Enborne. Everybody knows that a hundred years ago, there was not much trouble taken with the education of young ladies. The old saying goes, that a

11

little knowledge is a dangerous thing, and it really would seem as if parents endeavoured to keep from their daughters every portion of that element of mischief. A governess was unknown in parsonage houses, and even in country mansions, and was only heard of occasionally in the families of very great or wealthy people. Some girls *were* sent to school; but there was, with most fathers, a strong feeling against this, and I believe it was not a prejudice, but that the generality of girls' schools were very badly conducted. There were some exceptions in the last century, to this common state of ignorance. Mrs Montague, Mrs Carter, Mrs Vezey and others, may be named, as having been better scholars, and more deeply read than are ladies of the present day, but they *were* exceptions, and their example excited no emulation amongst the mass. They were more wondered at, than admired.[12]

The daughters of Enborne Parsonage got I believe about the average allowance of education, as bestowed at that time – certainly fully as much as their mother had ever received, tho' *she* was born in a higher position than they were. No language beyond their own was thought of and they learned *that* by ear; and tho' they spoke and wrote it with as few mistakes as did the younger and better-taught generation who afterwards grew up around them, I doubt if they could ever have assorted their words by any rules of grammar. Their mother taught them to read, and their first reading lesson, after the spelling book, was in the Psalms, considered to be easier than the other parts of Scripture. But *having* been taught to read, I fancy it was left afterwards very much to their own taste, what use they made of that acquirement; except that always a daily portion of the Psalms and Lessons was read in the family, and I believe something of history was got through. Some needlework was required daily, and they knitted all their own common stockings. They learnt of their mother to spin, but this was for their own amusement, it was not exacted; for the time had even *then* gone by, when it was any point of economy to have your linen woven from homespun flax. They also learnt, I suppose from their mother, to make pillow-lace. A master came regularly to teach writing and arithmetic.

As to accomplishments, if music had been desired, I suppose it would not have been very easy to find an instructor. For singing, none was thought needful. If girls had good voices, they *would* sing, like the birds, by nature, so what would be the use of teaching them? And if they had *not* voices, clearly it could be of no use at all. A young nightingale or lark, if you let it alone, would be sure to find its own song, but with all your teaching, you would never get a note worth hearing from a sparrow or a rook, so that point had not to be considered. The two eldest daughters had very good voices, one of them especially, with a most accurate ear. They liked to hear her sing, but I would answer for it, it never occurred to her parents that she had a talent which ought to be cultivated. Why should it be? – for she could catch any song from once hearing, and give it back in full rich soft tones, nothing could be pleasanter to listen to! I think she could have earned her livelihood as a ballad singer. What could teaching do for her? A master might injure her voice but he could not improve it. I am not drawing here entirely on my own invention tho' it is true I never heard Mr and Mrs Lloyd *so* express themselves – I could *not,* dates being considered – but I *do* remember opinions very similar prevailing in the family, and not in the family alone, and I have in early days heard old-fashioned people regret that such or such a one had had a singing-master – she sang so much better before!

But there was one grace and accomplishment which my grandmother *did* consider essential to the condition of a gentlewoman: a good air and carriage, and good dancing, and *this* was not trusted to nature, but for about seven years her daughters took a dancing lesson once a week at Newbury. Not seven continuous years – there was a break. They began very early, then left off for a time, and went on again for a year or so, in order to acquire a last finish, before they should be called on to open the Newbury Assemblies with a minuet in company with a few other young ladies of the neighbourhood. *This* over, the whole room afterwards danced merrily together country dances and cotillions, for the rest of the evening; so in preparation for *these,* and other similar occasions in their future lives, they were sent early in

13

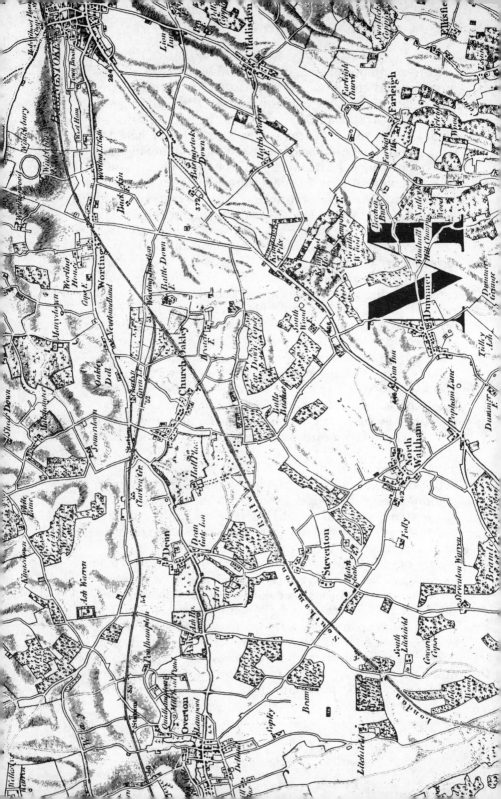

the day once a week to Mrs Hutchin's school in Northbrook Street, where the dancing master Mr Dore gave his attendance. It was a whole day of dancing. They began in the morning, stayed and dined with the schoolgirls, had another dancing lession in the evening, and after tea the carriage fetched them home. The trouble was not thrown away, for the desired end was attained, I have been told that they all danced well; and certainly, I know, that they all walked well, and I often heard this observation made, long after their youth had passed; and I think education, if it had been given, would have been attended with success also, on many other points.

I think their life at Enborne was, on *the whole,* a happy one. Their father's bad health precluded much company in their own house; but they had, from family connexions, a very good acquaintance in the neighbourhood, by which the young ladies naturally benefited. Whilst their father was equal to the exercise himself, they used to take long rides with him. Now and then, in a long summer's day, he would summon one of them to start early and ride with him to Bishopston. They had a rest there of some hours, whilst Mr Lloyd was engaged in parish business. They dined at the inn with the curate as a guest, and got back to Enborne in the evening. I do not know how many miles the distance was. After their father gave up riding, they seem always to have had horses at their command, tho' I do not suppose that the riding and the carriage horses were entirely distinct animals. They were considered good horsewomen, but in those days ladies were not expected to face many difficulties.

Of my grandfather Mr Lloyd, I must say a few words before I close the chapter of Enborne. He was a good scholar and divine, fond of literature, a writer of poetry himself, and a writer also of the sermons which he preached. *They* were accounted so good, that they were preserved and valued by the next generation – an extension of life very rarely granted to such compositions. I have heard several of them preached by my uncle Mr. Fowle. Their length was, I think, somewhere between 25 and 30 minutes. Mr Lloyd became a sad nervous invalid; generally keeping much in his own room, and some days equal to nothing. His malady had no name then; but I have heard it was thought afterwards, that it might have been suppressed gout. When better, he liked to amuse himself by playing at cards, and then his daughters were summoned to play with him. At first it was some childish game which they knew, for he was too nervous to teach them anything. But he was glad when he found that their mother had taught them whist, and afterwards they always played it. They played for money – some small stake I suppose – *he* always paying, whichever side might lose. Sometimes he would like backgammon, and then two were left at liberty. This constant card-playing was very irksome to three young girls, tho' to a degree it soothed his nervous sufferings.

He was, I believe, a good and a truly religious man; his daughters respected him, and thought highly of his abilities. But I fear he lived in their memories chiefly as a nervous hypochondriac, as the shadow cast over their young life. He died at Enborne, 28th January 1789, aged 69 years. His second daughter, Eliza, had previously married her cousin, the Revd Fulwar Craven Fowle, of Kintbury.[13] Mrs Lloyd, with her two other single daughters, took the parsonage house at Deane, renting it of my grandfather Mr Austen. After some time they removed to Ibthorp. From that house my mother was afterwards married in the church of Up Hurstbourne.[14]

From this long retrospect I return to the date of 1805. On 18th June I was born in the Rectory House of Steventon. Except, I suppose, to my own parents, that year was made more memorable by deaths, than by my birth. It was one of those seasons when the branches are shaken and the few remaining autumnal leaves fall to the ground. I have already noticed the deaths of Mr Austen and Mrs Lloyd and, a few months previously, those of Mr Craven and of a near neighbour and friend, Mrs Lefroy of Ashe; and on 26th December 1805 died, at Clanville, near Andover, General Mathew. *His* daughter Anne was my father's first wife, the mother of my sister Anna. Her own mother, Lady Jane Mathew, was a daughter of the Duke of Ancaster and sister to the last who bore that title. (Lady Jane Mathew died at Lainston House near Winchester, after her daughter Anne's marriage. The General was a widower when he took Clanville.)

16

At the time of my father's first marriage, General Mathew's family were living at Laverstoke, near Overton; not on the spot where stands the present Laverstoke House, but in a mansion of older date, at the bottom of the hill, near to the stream of water and not far from the road. In my remembrance the site could still be pointed out and something of old garden wall was standing. My father, when quite a young man, had the curacy of Overton, and *then* and *there* and *so* it was, I suppose, that the attachment was formed, and the marriage was concluded. He then left the very small vicarage house, where he had lived as a single man and took Court House, still in the parish. I do not know *when* he and his wife moved to Deane; but eventually that was their home; and there she died, rather suddenly, after but a few years of married life, leaving only one daughter [Anna]. My father remained on at Deane; he was my grandfather's curate there. He married again and my brother was born at Deane. The intimacy with the Mathews continued more than might have been expected, under the circumstances, for the General was one of my brother's godfathers. My mother was a frequent guest at Clanville, and was treated with great consideration by General Mathew, but said she never could get over the fear of him; he was a man whose word was undisputed law to his whole family.

In 1801 Mr and Mrs Austen with their two daughters had left Steventon, and settled themselves at Bath. My father then began his residence at the Rectory House, Steventon, and acted as my grandfather's curate for Deane also, till 1805. Then, on my grandfather's death, Steventon became his own – the reversion of it having been left to him by Mr Knight – and all connection with Deane ceased.

1806

The General was buried on 1st January; I see that my father went to Clanville for the funeral and stayed several days. On 13th January died Mr Lefroy – he did not long survive his wife. My father buried him on the 20th. Mr Fowle died, aged 79, on 7th February; he was buried on the 12th, and that same evening died his son Charles. This was at

17

Kintbury Vicarage, where my uncle and aunt Fowle lived, the old Mr. Fowle remaining their inmate, after resigning the living in favour of his son. He retained till his death the small preferment of Hampstead [Marshall] and performed the service as usual in that church, the Sunday before he died.

In consequence of the death of old Mr Fowle my father was asked to hold the living of Hampstead [Marshall] for some years, until the young man for whom it was designed should be of age to take it. It is only lately that I heard how this happened. Lord Craven, the patron, asked Mr Fowle, with whom he was on intimate terms, and a near neighbour, to look out for him 'an honest man', who would take the living now and give it up at the appointed time. He had, he said, been once deceived by a clergyman to whom he had given a valuable living on condition that he should only hold it for a young friend; and that when the time came, he refused to resign it.

The value of this [living] was small, but it would have made a very welcome addition to my father's income – yet he hesitated; not from any fear that he should be tempted to retain it dishonestly beyond the appointed time, but solely on account of the *words* which must be used in accepting it. He did not deem the arrangement simoniacal in spirit; but *there* stood the ugly word; and he doubted whether a *promise* to give up, at a certain time, did not go against the *letter* of the declaration which he would have to make.[15] The very few whom he consulted could not see it as *he* did; and willing to give himself every chance of conviction, I know he went to London to lay his scruples before someone of high authority in ecclesiastical matters, and to ask an opinion. But the difficulty still remained the same to him. In vain was he told, and in vain did he tell himself, that livings *had* been so held by very good men; that occasions frequently occurred when such service was greatly needed, and must he then believe that it was always wrongfully given? – that the patron who offered was the tempter, and the priest who accepted was the sinner who fell into the snare? – was it reasonable or charitable to suppose this?

Yet still he made answer to himself, that *he* must be guided by his own conscience. To those 'who doubted not' there could be no sin imputed, but *he* could not see his way so clearly. It appears from the entries in the pocket-book, that he took one week to make up his mind – and then declined to hold the living. It was a period I doubt not of very anxious and painful deliberation. If Lord Craven ever knew the reason of the refusal, he must have despaired of ever getting the right man for his purpose – having found one with too little conscience, and another with too much. But probably he was never told more than that it would not suit Mr Austen to take the living. I cannot but observe that there was no scruple then about pluralities. My father was a pluralist, in a small way; and in reading memoirs of the strictest of men, the evangelical clergy, it is clear that they saw no objection to the practice of holding two livings.

July 2nd 'The Honble Mrs Mary Leigh of Stoneleigh died'.[16] I find no family event recorded after this, in 1806, but there is a notice of the election for the county, thus: 'The Poll began on Monday November 10th and on Thursday the 13th Chute and Mildmay gave up to Herbert and Thistlethwaite'.

1807

In 1807 my mother had a most painful illness from an abscess in the face. March 7th, she took to her room, and on 16th June 'dined downstairs' – there is no other notice of it. I had always believed that I myself remembered a circumstance connected with her sufferings; but as the date shews that I was not then two years old, I suppose it is impossible and that it must have been mentioned to me afterwards.

1808

March 6th 'John Bond's house was burnt down'. *This* I have certainly always remembered distinctly – I was not three years old.[17]

June 13th My father and mother, taking my brother and myself, and Mary Smallbone who then lived with us, went to Godmersham. We had gone to London the day before. We stayed rather more than three weeks and on our way back, spent one whole day at Bookham in Surrey, the Revd [Samuel] Cooke's. On the Saturday that we came back, there is this entry in the pocket-book: 'Returned home; and all glad to find ourselves at Steventon again; tho' we had spent our time very pleasantly'.[18]

I remember the Godmersham visit well, in many little points; and I don't think I *was* very happy there, in a strange house. I recollect the model of a ship in a passage, and my cousins' rabbits out of doors, in or near a long walk of high trees. I have been told it was the lime-tree walk. As I never visited the place again, the very little that I *do* remember, must date from that time. It was in this same year of 1808 that there came the sad change over my uncle's life, and Godmersham lost its mistress.

October 10th 'Mrs Edward Austen died suddenly'. She was supposed to be recovering very well after the birth of her eleventh child – a son. On the 12th, as soon as the tidings came, my mother went to Winchester and fetched away Edward and George. They stayed till the 22nd and then went back to school. Nobody seemed to have thought of their going home. Long distances appeared then unsurmountable difficulties.[19]

1809

Nothing very notable in the early part of the year – only my mother spent about a month with her sister-in-law Mrs Frank Austen at Alton, awaiting her confinement. Captain Austen was at sea. I remember her absence from home, and that I was left under the care of my sister, but I had no idea she had been away so long.[20] Whilst she was there, my grandmother and aunts on July 7th took possession of their new home at Chawton. They moved from Southampton.

On Monday 28th August my father and mother, my brother and myself, attended this time by Betsy Smallbone, began our journey to Stoneleigh Abbey. We slept at Mrs Craven's, Speen Hill, and the next day we reached Stoneleigh soon after 8 o'clock in the evening. Stoneleigh was then occupied by the Revd Thomas Leigh, an elderly

man, a widower without children, and with him lived his
elderly sister, Miss Elizabeth Leigh. Very good and kind
people they were, as I have always heard, but of them personally I do not remember much, nor would my testimony
to their goodness be worth anything, even were my recollections of them more distinct. He had come into possession of
the Stoneleigh estates on the death of the Honble Miss Mary
Leigh in 1806. He had before resided in his parsonage house
at Adlestrop [Glos.], which he and his sister left with great
regret, and they never thoroughly enjoyed their promotion
to Stoneleigh. The change came too late in their lives to be
pleasant to them. He retained his living, for which the present generation would scarcely find words strong enough to
express their censure, that he and his sister might still spend
some part of the year in the old parsonage they loved so well.
I am sure from his general character it was not for the emolu-
ment. I do not think there were any scruples then about non-
residence if the duties of the church were properly performed. Of course Mr Leigh provided a curate. I do not
know how the money affairs were arranged, but from his
well-known character, I feel sure that nobody was the worse
for the attachment he bore to his old home.

I remember nothing of the journey, but well recollect our
arrival there. As we passed under an archway, a deep bell
gave notice of our approach. I believe it was the porter's
lodge. We had come in late, at 8 o'clock. I remember it was
dark, and that the lights seemed very bright as we drove up
to the house, and the servants were waiting to receive us. We
entered a room on the right-hand side of the hall. There were
many people in it, and tea was going on and bread-and-milk
was brought for me. Then as it was assumed I ought to go to
bed at once, the mistress of the house undertook to conduct
us upstairs. That Miss Elizabeth never felt quite at home in
Stoneleigh Abbey was proved the evening of our arrival,
when she wandered about the house trying in vain to dis-
cover *what* room had been prepared for me and my maid.
She *knew* she had ordered it to be near my mother's, but she
could not find either apartment. I remember seeing her turn
down the bedclothes in several rooms, to see if there were
sheets on the bed. At last she felt obliged to ask my mother

if I could sit up till after prayers, and then she would get one of the housemaids to show the room. No difficulty was made and I went to prayers. They were read by Mr Leigh twice a day in the chapel where he had all the family assemble – the time in the evening was 9 o'clock. Afterwards my room was quickly found. Miss Elizabeth had only gone up the wrong staircase.

I see by the pocket-book, and I also remember the names, tho' not much of the personages, that Lady Saye and Sele and Lady and Miss Hawke were staying in the house.

I think I was very happy at Stoneleigh. Nobody teized me, or wanted me much in the parlour, and I had the range of the house, with Betsy for my companion. The size of the rooms and the antique appearance of some of them impressed me very much. I delighted chiefly in the picture gallery, as it was called, tho' not many pictures were there; but in it stood a spinett, so old and uncared for, that I was allowed to play on it as much as I pleased. From the gallery, a double flight of stone steps descended into the garden. This gallery was in the old Abbey part of the house, and you entered it from the modern part, through two rooms – one called the state bedroom – and a short staircase made the communication with the gallery.

In these two apartments, the bed and the old furniture remained, but they were never used, you only passed through them to get to the gallery. It had been hoped in the year '45, that Prince Charles Edward would have occupied them for at least one night; but he was not destined to enjoy such comfortable quarters in England; and I have heard it said it was very fortunate for the Leighs that he retreated without reaching the midland counties.

There was another long low room in the old part of the house, called the print gallery, the walls being covered with, I believe, very ordinary prints. I used to have my dinner, with Betsy, in the housekeeper's room, to which we made our way along a vaulted passage. I think all the offices were in the old building. There was a chapel, and Mr Leigh read prayers in it twice a day – in the morning at 9 o'clock. I believe the chapel was in the more modern part of the house.

Excursions were made most days to see something:

Warwick Castle, Guy's Cliff, Combe Abbey and Kenilworth were visited. And here I must relate, what I never forgot, my brother's great good nature to his little sister. *He* made one in all these parties, therefore I saw but little of him, and at last when I heard he was going off again *that* morning to Kenilworth, I burst out crying, and complained, I believe, that he was always away from me; and he instantly said, he would stay at home, and play with me instead, and this he *did*. I believed at the time, and for long afterwards, that they went to see some sort of dog kennel. One day he went to Warwick Races, with some of the party from the house. Mr Leigh was not amongst them, and a visitor's carriage was used, for he would not suffer his own to appear on the course, deeming it improper that a clergyman's equipage should be seen there. This of course I only learnt long afterwards. His objections must have been thought odd at that time, when scruples as to worldly amusements were not very commonly heard of, except amongst the evangelical clergy and *their* followers. Mr Thomas Leigh did not belong to the rising evangelical party, but was, I believe, what was then called a High Churchman. I suppose it was on this occasion that Lady Saye and Sele, who had stayed at home, complained that her aunt (Miss Elizabeth) had taken her up into her dressing-room, and read a sermon to her. Such a very odd day, she said, to read a sermon!

September 8th   'We left Stoneleigh, and slept at Oxford; and the next day, Saturday, we got home; calling at Speen on the Mrs Hulberts'.

I have always remembered Stoneleigh much more fully than Godmersham. I was a year older and the place made a great impression on me. I doubted at last, whether I *did* really remember it so well, or whether it was partly fancy – but in the year 1833 I was taken there again by friends who called in travelling to see the place, the family being absent; and there I found all as I recollected it to have been. I knew my way to the picture gallery and looked for the old spinett, and found it just where I had left it, only it had lost all power of sound. The place I then saw *was* the very same Stoneleigh Abbey I had so long remembered; save and except, that the apartments were not so large nor the galleries quite so long

23

and so noble as they had appeared to the child of four years old.[21]

This year was the Jubilee – the 50th complete of George 3rd's reign.

October 24th 'Went to a Ball at Basingstoke, in honour of His Majesty'.

October 25th 'Gave a dinner in Mr Digweed's barn, to all the poor of the parish'.

Nothing more to note in this year, until in December all went to stay at Mrs Hulbert's – my father and brother but a few days, I stayed on with my mother. Then occurred a serious illness of Mrs Hulbert's, of which I remember something, and that I was transferred to Mrs Craven's house, my mother staying on to help nurse her old friend – my father returned for a day or two. On the last day of December: 'Mrs Hulbert pronounced out of danger'.

1810

We began the year at Speen and we did not get home till the 20th January. My father was backwards and forwards from Steventon. During the remainder of this year, I see but a repetition of small home engagements. Believing that we had always lived a very retired life, I have been surprised to find, in looking over these little books, how very little we were alone. Not very often parties, but two or three to dinner and relations frequently staying in the house, and it appears to have been as much the custom then as it is now, that neighbours should be invited to meet home guests. The names of Lefroy, Digweed, Terry, Harwood, Wither and Heathcote, come over the most frequently. My father often dined at The Vine, my mother but seldom, and staying the night, if she did go.

My Uncle Edward, as we then called him – he had not taken the name of Knight – came to Chawton and Steventon generally twice a year to look after his affairs. He must have been more his own 'man of business' than is usual with people of large property, for I think it was his greatest interest to attend to his estates. In my recollection, he never hunted or shot. He liked riding and made his horse the means of getting about, sometimes coming to us in this manner from Chawton, if alone, a little roll behind the saddle, bringing necessaries enough for a night or two. But about this period, I see he was frequently accompanied by some of his family – a daughter and a Miss Deedes, or a Miss Cage.[22] Of the five brothers, *he,* who had always had unlimited means for such indulgence, was the only one without a strong taste for field sports, and *he* cared not for them at all. He was very cheerful and pleasant, and had some of my Aunt Jane's power and good nature, of telling amusing stories to his nephews and nieces.

In December my sister went to stay with her uncle and aunt, Mr and Mrs Mathew, at Clanville, which they rented for only a short time, and she was there several weeks. This Mr Mathew succeeded many years later to very great wealth, and most unexpectedly. It was in consequence of the death of a young relation, the Honble Mr Collyer, who travelling in Italy, was attacked by banditti, and tho' I think he escaped alive out of their hands, the wounds proved fatal.

1811

The first month of this year, on 30th January, it is noted 'Edward's pony died suddenly'. I saw its dying struggles in the stable, having been taken out there by one of the maids, who hurried me off again directly. This was a great grief to my brother, and some to me. Pony was sorrowfully interred in a corner of the Home Meadow, and his grave was discernible for some years afterwards.

My mother's picture was taken this year – greatly against her own will. It was a miniature by a Mr Jackson, who came round the neighbourhood on speculation. This was in May.[23]

In July, on the 4th, the deceased favourite's place was supplied by another pony, called Sutton. He lived on with us many years, and was a most useful animal, carrying anybody on the road, and taking his young master with the hounds. Just at this time were begun great alterations about the place; new stables built, and much improvement made in the approach to the house.

In November Captain Charles Austen came, bringing his wife whom he had married in Bermuda; it was the first time that I can recollect having seen him. I was much charmed with both – but thought they looked very young for an uncle and aunt – tho' she must then have been the mother of two children. She was fair and pink, with very light hair, and I admired her greatly. They stayed but three days; and that was all I ever saw of her. She had no opportunity of coming to Steventon again. My uncle's profession did not, in those times, allow of much holiday on shore, and her life was a short one. She died at The Nore, where her husband had the guard ship, immediately after the birth of her fourth child, who did not long survive her.[24]

1812

In June, my grandmother, Mrs Austen, and Aunt Jane, spent more than a fortnight with us at Steventon. I cannot find again any notice of a visit from Mrs Austen, and I conclude this was the last time she ever came. I have heard that when she determined to go no more from her own house she said her last visit should be to her eldest son – and that accordingly she came, and made her farewell to the place where [the] most part of her own married life had been spent. She kept her resolution, and as I believe, never again left Chawton for a single night.

On 12th August my brother went to school, at Mr Meyrick's of Ramsbury, my father taking him there, and staying a night at Kintbury.

October 14th 'Mrs Knight died'. She was the widow of the Mr Thomas Knight who had left all his property to my Uncle Edward, after *her* death. They had adopted him and brought him up as a son. When he should come into possession, at her death, he was to take the name of Knight, but very soon after she became a widow she gave up everything to him, reserving an income of £2,000 a year for herself. She settled in Canterbury, and there died. On her decease, according to Mr Knight's Will, the change of name took place; but my uncle had been the representative of the Knights at Godmersham many years previously, owing to

View of Steventon from Barley Lane.
(A nineteenth-century water-colour, probably by Julia Lefroy.)

Deane House.

her generous resignation in his favour.

Through this year of 1812 the usual names of friends and neighbours appear on the pages of the pocket-book. We went several times to stay – we were at Kintbury, Speen and Chawton. Also I notice, and this agrees with my own recollections, that in my father's absences for a night or two at Chawton, or elsewhere, my mother indulged herself in drinking tea with some of her neighbours – most frequently it was with the Harwoods at Deane – taking me with her.

1813

On 11th January, died our near neighbour, Mr Harwood of Deane, an old man. He left a widow, his sister lived with them, and his eldest son, a clergyman, had always made his home there. The family party never separated. The son became the master, and his mother continued the nominal mistress, in whose name the household affairs were conducted. But the *real* manageress was 'My Aunt', Mrs Anna Harwood, and very well she *did* manage the affairs of that impoverished family, to whom the closest daily economy suddenly became not only a virtue, but a necessity. On the death of the old man sad disclosures came to light, and ruin stared them in the face. The property at Deane was worth about £1,200 a year and it had descended through a squirearchy of John Harwoods, fathers and sons, for five or six generations, but it was *so* to descend no longer. Old Mr Harwood had contracted debts, quite unsuspected by his family. He had borrowed and mortgaged so freely, that it seemed as if the estate itself could scarcely pay its own liabilities. There was nothing for his widow, and his sister's small portion had been left in his hands, and had gone with the rest of the money, so that both ladies were dependent on the heir. He found himself a ruined man on his father's death, blighted in all his hopes and prospects of life, whatever they might have been, and they were pretty well guessed at. It was generally supposed, I believe I might say, it was generally known amongst his intimate friends, that he had formed an attachment to a lady of good position in his own neighbourhood. It was also believed, though not of course

27

with equal certainty, that this lady, a widow, and quite her own mistress, would be willing to accept him. Nor could it have been considered a bad match for *her*, if, on his father's death he could have offered her, as he had a right to expect, a home in the family mansion with an estate of at least £1,000 a year around it. But, as I have said before, he then found himself a ruined man, and bound to provide as best he could for his mother and aunt.

The love to which I have referred, though sincere and strong, I believe, on both sides, was not of that romantic, youthful nature, which foresees no evil in poverty, and in the change of social position that is sure to follow. The lady had been accustomed to all the comforts of life, and also she had a young son to care for, and for his sake, even if not for her own, she would feel it both unfitting and unseemly to enter into a ruined family; and the gentleman probably having his own full share of proper pride, refrained from offering his 'nothing' to her acceptance. The friendship continued; each was for long an object of much interest to the other, but varied circumstances brought other interests and other cares to both. Time did his office in smoothing and obliterating and a tranquil good will attended their latter years.[25]

Having crushed and buried his hope, not of his youth but of his mature manhood, one desire was left to reign supreme. He had the strong hereditary feeling of attachment to the soil, which, as it cannot be explained or accounted for by any arguments of reason, deserves we must suppose to die out of the world, as it *is* fast dying out; and to be remembered only (if at all) as a prejudice, happily extinct. He had a certain pride, nor could anything have convinced him that it was pride improper, in being the representative of a line of English squires, of no great estate, he knew, but who had lived upon their own property on the same spot, and handed it down from father to son for five or six generations. I believe he was himself the first heir who had ever chosen to go into any profession – he was a clergyman. To make a struggle still to keep the estate together for his successor; to leave a John Harwood in the old house at Deane – though *that* John Harwood would not be his own son – this seemed to him the duty that he owed to the past and to the future, and to this, he resolved to sacrifice the present. Yet I do not say it was all self-sacrifice. He loved every nook and corner about the place and felt that if the old walls could still shelter him and his, every privation, short of actual want under his own roof, could be endured, and would be preferable to a life of more ease in any other abode; that a dinner of herbs at Deane would be sweeter than a stalled ox eaten elsewhere, with the bitter sauce of alienation. It might not have been so, but he never made the trial when the choice was before him; for he might, by selling off the estate, have at once paid off the mortgages and the debts and some little money would have remained to him which with his *very* small clerical income might have maintained the family in tolerable comfort, in some small dwelling, near one of the churches that he served; and *so* as other people thought, his mind would have been made easier and the daily burden of enforced economy need not have been so heavy on the household. To this course all his friends advised him and so hopeless seemed the case to them that when they found that he was determined to 'hold on', he was generally blamed, as sacrificing too much to hereditary attachment; even *then,* when the feeling *was* understood and when it commanded more respect and sympathy, than it would now receive. But he *did* prevail on himself to sell a small portion of land to a neighbour who much desired to have it to throw into his own grounds, and who gave therefore a fancy price. Whether he was willing to pay more for it than such fancies may fairly cost a rich man, I do not know, but I *can* say that his wife unfeignedly rejoiced over the large sum which then found its way into Mr Harwood's hands, which was advantageously employed in satisfying some of the most pressing claims.

February 24th   Mr Wither of Manydown died. On 3rd March my father attended his funeral.[26]

April 24th   Mrs Henry Austen died in London – my Uncle Henry's first wife. I do not remember that I ever saw her.[27]

In this year, 1813, my uncle Mr Knight came, with all his family, to spend the summer at Chawton House. We stayed with them there in May.

At the end of October I went with my mother to Kintbury,

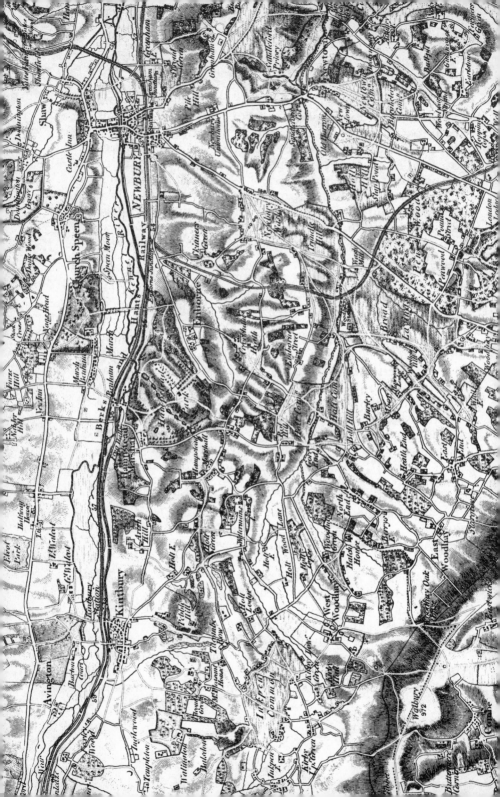

to join ourselves to their larger party, and to proceed all together to Cheltenham. My Aunt Fowle, my three cousins and ourselves, got there November 1st, a long day's journey from Kintbury. We had a house first in Bedford Place, and then in St George's Square. My uncle and his eldest son joined us later on. I believe most of the party went for their health – still nobody was an invalid – and I think there was a good deal of quiet gaiety amongst the grown-up people, and we children had the amusement of looking about us. Mr and Mrs Fowle had once lived at Elkstone. He still retained the living, and several of their old friends yet remained in the neighbourhood, and some new acquaintances were made in Cheltenham. Amongst them were Doctor and Mrs Jenner, and in consequence of something that passed in conversation Dr Jenner offered to re-vaccinate me. He thought, from what he was told of my vaccination that I was not inevitably safe. I had therefore the honour of a second operation from the hands of the great discoverer himself; and at the end of the whole process, he pronounced it had been all right before. He was at this time an elderly man, and had, I suppose, retired from practice. We stayed at Cheltenham till 6th December and then came home, sleeping one night at Mrs Hulbert's. We left the other party, and *their* stay was lengthened beyond their intention by a heavy fall of snow, after Christmas, which made the roads impassable for a long time. This was the hard winter of '13 and '14. Charles Fowle spent his holidays with us from Winchester.

1814

In the summer of this year, I had the great pleasure of a friend and companion for a short time in Hester Wheeler, a girl of about thirteen, whom Mrs Chute had brought to The Vine about a twelvemonth before.[28] I had heard a great deal of her from my brother and had long had a great wish to see her. I had, myself, but little intercourse with The Vine, but from my father and brother's being so often there, I seemed to know a great deal about the family. I was over-joyed when I heard Hester was really coming to stay at Steventon, and it fell out thus. Mrs Chute had perhaps at

31

first intended to educate her herself, as she was an inmate of the house for several months; but if *so*, she changed her plan, and sent her to school at Winchester. The summer holidays were come, and Hester had only just recovered from the measles. There was a fear of infection both at The Vine and at Oakley Hall, and my father, hearing Mrs Chute say she was afraid she must keep her at Winchester a week or two longer, begged she might come to Steventon at once — and so she came. To me she was a very delightful companion, the first I had ever felt really fond of, and it seemed afterwards as if our intimacy must have lasted much longer than the twelve days, which I see was the term of her visit, so deep was the impression she made on me. Long before, I had eagerly listened to her history, all that I could hear of it, and *how* it was that she came to be at The Vine. I believe it was Hester's great-aunt, who had once been governess to the Miss Chutes — I fancy what would now be called a nursery governess. I suppose she remained long in the house, for Mrs Chute and Mrs Bramston seemed to acknowledge a strong claim of charity towards the family. They were in very humble life, as Hester never sought to conceal. They must have at one time kept a shop, for she has told me of a recollection of standing on her grandmother's counter. I think they lived in Norwich. This grandmother was Mrs Marshall, and one of her daughters, Hester's mother, was singularly beautiful; and unhappily a Captain Wheeler, stationed in the town, fell in some sort of love with her, and married her. He also deserted her, a few months afterwards, before Hester's birth, and he never reappeared. In time it came to be rumoured that he was a married man when first he made her acquaintance, and even that Wheeler was not his real name — but nobody ever knew. How much his young wife had loved him, and how much she grieved for him, as I never heard I will not pretend to say; but she was left in sad straits and difficulties, and had to seek a maintenance for herself and her child, and leaving the little girl with her relations, she entered the family of Mr Beach as governess to his daughter. The position was different then from what it is now; for she acted as lady's maid to my Aunt Mrs Fowle, when she was staying with Mr and Mrs Beach at Netheravon. I ought to say that the service was quite voluntary on her part. Mrs Wheeler so entreated to be allowed to come every day and dress her that my aunt was obliged to consent; but said it distressed her to be waited on by such a pretty ladylike young woman. She thought her also remarkably pleasing in manner. Her health soon failed, and she fell into a decline. Then Mr and Mrs Chute received her at The Vine, and there she was tenderly nursed during the short remainder of her life, Mrs Chute attending on her to the last. They had her little girl also in the house, a child about three years old.

Afterwards, when that little girl was a grown-up woman, she wrote an affecting account of these last days, as she had had them related to her. It was published, though without the names, in some periodical of the day. I believe there was no exaggeration; *I* had heard the tale also from eye-witnesses. It was in the Red Room at The Vine that Mrs Wheeler died. The beauty of the dying woman remained unimpaired to the end, as is not unusual in consumptive cases. The devotion of her attendants, the picturesque chamber, the bright summer sun, and the sweet roses clustering round the open windows, made the picture; then there were the words of prayer, the last farewells, the passing away of the spirit, the countenance of the dead, which spoke of peace and rest at last; all this the daughter loved to think on, and had a satisfaction in recording, as best she might. It was the only tribute she could pay to her mother's memory.

Mrs Wheeler must have been unusually gifted with grace and beauty. Ladies liked her and approved of her, and gentlemen fell in love with her. Her position was very humble, and so was her birth and nobody quite knew – she did not know herself – whether she was legally bound as the wife of Captain Wheeler, or whether he had had a wife living at the time he married her, and in those days, if he had only married under a false name, I believe the marriage would have been void.

Notwithstanding these clouds of doubt and difference of station, more than one was deeply enamoured of her. I could mention their names, but I shall not. All has passed away so long that, as individuals, I will not call up their memories. I

33

allude to them only as their admiration made a part of the history of Mrs Wheeler's short life. She had been apparently raised in station by her supposed marriage with an officer in the army; then, as the deserted, penniless wife, or perhaps no wife at all, she fell lower than before, and then again came the triumph of beauty, reaching her in her very subordinate position. The events of life were not exhausted for her. I know nothing of her own feelings; I never heard them even guessed at. It might have been only fresh grief that awaited her, but it might have been great prosperity, and then came the triumph of death over all! Beauty, sorrow, hopes and regrets, received into the cloud of oblivion; and such a tangled skein had been the web of her life, that even those who loved her best, could not long have regretted her early death; and 'so best' must have been the conviction of all who loved her, when the first feeling of grief had passed away.

A good deal of this was known to Hester, at the time of which I am writing, enough to make her feel she had received from her mother 'a heritage of woe'; but then she felt, I think, that she had received also a heritage of beauty and romance. She must have been very pretty – everybody said so, and some called her beautiful – but those who had known Mrs Wheeler did not fail to add that she could never be equal to her mother; and *this* I think pleased her too, for somehow such sayings came round to her, and she made an idol of her mother's memory. I have little recollection of her face at this time. She was scarcely thirteen but was generally taken for fifteen at least. She was very clever, quick in learning everything, and Mrs Chute had found her a very pleasant pupil. I am sure she was not conceited; children never fail to find out *that* bad quality, if it exists; nor do I remember that she cared about dress; nor did she seem at all occupied with her own beauty, tho' aware of it.

She was good-natured and lively; and altho' older than myself by at least three years, she did not assume any airs of eldership. She had a very affectionate manner, naturally caressing, and perhaps she seemed to love you more than she did; but she *was* really fond of all who were kind to her. The Chutes, the Bramstons and Caroline Wiggett seemed always near her heart. She knew clearly her own condition in life, and that she must be a governess; and she expected she should die early, like her mother, and of the same malady. But tho' she would speak of all this freely – she had excellent spirits – the prospects of the future did not depress her. She was ready for everything; she liked rambling about with me, getting wild flowers; and a swing in the barn, a ride on the donkey, or above all, on the pony, she enjoyed like a child; such as she was in years, tho' scarcely in appearance. She was very enlivening to me; and perhaps the one great charm was her variety of talk – occasionally on sad or serious subjects, and then in high glee over anything, or nothing.

It was a blank day to me when she passed on to Oakley Hall, but we met again several times in these holidays, and also at Christmas, when she came from The Vine and there were little parties at Mrs Bramston's and at our house. But a sudden revolution soon afterwards closed our intercourse. Poor Hester, with all her charmingness, was far from perfect. She was self-willed and she could be rebellious, and before the next summer holidays came round, serious differences arose between her and her school mistress, differences which were terminated by Hester's walking away from Kingsgate Street altogether. She took the road to Popham Lane, the next stage about ten miles on, intending, I believe, to walk all the way – a daring exploit for any girl. Her object was the inn there, kept by the Biggs. Two of the daughters had been her schoolfellows at Winchester, and she was sure they would take her in. I do not know how far she had walked, when she was overtaken by a return chaise belonging to the same inn. Perhaps she was getting tired, or frightened, and was glad to finish her journey on easier terms, and the chaise conveyed her to the Biggs' house. They received her, of course, and immediately sent to apprise Mrs Bramston of what had happened. The particulars I never knew, only that she was taken back to The Vine, and was considered to be 'en penitence', but 'penitent', in English, I do not think she *was*. I saw her only once after this, for a short space, at Oakley Hall, as our further intercourse was discouraged on all sides. I remember I asked her, how she came to run away from school; and she answered 'because it was impossible to stay'. She was shortly afterwards sent back to Norfolk. Education had not prospered in Hampshire, and it was, I suppose, still conducted elsewhere. The subject was never mentioned, after just the first. Mrs Chute must have been greatly disappointed at the failure of her kind plan; and probably this escapade of Hester's raised anxious thoughts as to her future life and conduct. Her story shall be finished now, tho' it must carry me far beyond my date of 1814. It was not till 1820 that our attention was called to her again. Then we learnt that her friends were seeking a situation for her, as governess; and one was quickly found with a family in Berkshire. She was then about nineteen. She gave great satisfaction, and at Christmas she spent her holidays at The Vine, and in returning, she came to see us once more. We were then occupying Mrs Hulbert's house at Speen for the winter. With great interest I awaited Hester's arrival. She entered – so altered, in growing up, that we should neither of us have known her again from the first glance. The peculiar beauty of her childhood was gone; and those who had said then, that she would never equal her mother – though they spoke probably at random – were proved to have made a right guess. Yet she had a striking and intelligent countenance, and with a tall full-formed figure she was certainly a very fine young woman, who could scarcely pass unnoticed anywhere. She looked five- or six-and-twenty. Her manner was less changed than her face. There was the same affectionate warmth, the same facility of saying the things that it was most pleasant to hear. I was very desirous to renew our former friendship and so was she; and there were plans made for further intercourse, but they were not to be carried out. That short interview was the last, and we never met again. Dates fail me here, and I cannot tell exactly how long she remained in Berkshire. There was much in her nature, sadly at variance with the duties of her station. She was not fitted to encounter the troubles and trials of governess life. There was great dissatisfaction in the family, and she left them, returning to her relations in Norfolk, and she remained there some time, her health being bad. At length, we heard she had gone with a family, as governess, into Scotland; and, not long afterwards, that she was married at Dundee to a Mr George Duncan, a linen-draper of that town. He fell in love, by seeing her at church – and on making some acquaintance, found I suppose that there was no great barrier between a thriving tradesman and a poor wandering penniless governess – and soon brought her home to his house. Mrs Chute, and all her friends in England heard with much satisfaction that she had gained a home of her own. Hester's letters, after she married, spoke of great happiness. She wrote to me several times. She seemed very much attached to her husband. A few years passed – I cannot remember how many – but enough to introduce one subject of regret. She had no children, and this was touched on sometimes, as the *one* blessing which was withheld. She had, she said, everything else that she could desire. In a few more years she may have felt glad that this ever doubtful blessing *had* been denied. Her health failed, and she perceived the approach of that complaint which she had so long ago foretold for herself. She fell into a decline, and after a lingering, tho' I believe not a very suffering illness, she passed away, as her mother had passed before her, whilst still young!

The only old friend who ever saw her after her marriage was Miss Smith (Aunt Emma).[29] Her wanderings took her into Scotland, and she resolved to visit Dundee and see the Duncans. She gave a consoling account of poor Hester who knew full well her own hopeless state, and talked of the past, the present and the future, with the feelings that were most to be desired. She was very grateful for the visit, and the report of this interview gave much satisfaction to those who used to know and love her. I chanced to be at The Vine when Mrs Chute received the intelligence of her death. Mr Duncan came there for a few days, as a visitor, some time afterwards, and my brother happened to meet him. He was a man of good manners and appearance and, as it seemed, of good education; but what was the most striking, was the intimate knowledge he had, of all the places and people connected with Hester's young Hampshire days. He had begged to be allowed to come to The Vine, that he might know the friend who had done so much for her and see the place that she had loved to talk of. He appeared to know all whom she had known; asked after me by my name; knew where we had lived, and would have liked to see Steventon himself; but it was too far for a convenient drive, and he would not have found much of the Steventon left that she had known. Poor Hester had an affectionate heart, and had dwelt fondly on the recollection of all early friends, and he had evidently given her his full sympathy, in listening to all she liked to relate, and had thrown himself into her past life, for the love that he bore to her. In all her letters she had mentioned him with affection and gratitude. The last period of her life had been the happiest, and *he* had made it so! Peace be to her memory – peace, but not quite oblivion yet!

In the October of this year, 1814, we first heard that Mr Knight was threatened with the loss of much of his property. The heirs-at-law laid claim to it. They were the Baverstocks of Alton, and the Hintons, then living in the village of Chawton. This affair dragged on for a year or two, and was at last compromised by my uncle paying them £30,000. This it was, I believe, which occasioned the great gap in Chawton Park Wood, visible for thirty years afterwards, and probably not filled up again even now. I will here write down some particulars, which I never knew till in later days. They were given by the Revd Arthur Loveday, at the request of my sister, his mother-in-law, who, like myself, had never clearly understood on *what* the claim rested. Arthur Loveday's grandmother, Mrs Wells, had been a Miss Hinton, another Miss Hinton was Mrs Ventris, and they had a brother, John Hinton. These three were all in the position of claimants, but Mrs Wells and her husband declined taking any part in the proceedings.

From the Revd Arthur Loveday: 'In Mrs Knight's Will there were three persons mentioned in the entail of the Chawton property: first, Mr Lloyd, solicitor of Newbury; second, Mr May, also solicitor of Newbury; third, John Hinton. On May succeeding he and his son cut off the entail, and the younger May devised the property by Will, as you know, to young Austen, whom they had adopted. (The Mays took the name of Knight on coming into the property.) Subsequently an endeavour was made to prove a flaw in the cutting-off of the entail – which ended in a compromise.[30]

The large sum paid down by Mr Knight to settle the matter, was, I believe, chiefly swallowed up by the lawyers. What was left was divided, not equally, amongst the Baverstocks, Dusautoys, and Hintons. Baverstock was a clever and rather scampish brewer of Alton, whose Father had married Mr Hinton's daughter by his first wife; she had a good fortune, and as *he* chiefly promoted the suit, and bore the risk, he came in for a large share of the spoil. Mrs Ventris, my mother's aunt, Mr Hinton's youngest daughter by his second wife, contributed to the law expenses all she had won in the lottery. Mrs Dusautoy, the eldest sister, got something; the other sister, my grandmother (Mrs Wells), nothing, I believe, as she had not taken part in the affair. The son whom you know as "Jack Hinton" I suppose must have received something, but it could have been but trifling. The father, or grandfather, of Mr Hinton the clergyman, was a solicitor at Newbury also; but their pedigree is believed to be good. I have understood that the property would have come to them by descent after Mrs Elizabeth Knight, had she not left it by Will first to the Mays. I remember that the claim of the Baverstocks and Hintons rested on their being able to prove the informality of the deed by which the entail had been cut off. One flaw was said to be that it had been executed out of term-time. The intention of the testator, Mr Knight, to make Edward Austen his heir, was never disputed'.

On 8th November my sister was married to Benjamin Lefroy, Esq.[31] He had not then taken Orders, although of the full age that was necessary. Weddings were then usually very quiet. The old fashion of festivity and publicity had quite gone by, and was universally condemned as showing the great bad taste of all former generations. But never let today boast itself as being so much wiser than yesterday, for tomorrow may, most probably, bring the same folly back again; and that of the wedding feast, if it be a folly, has been since revived and is now flourishing, and no protest is now ever heard against it. My sister's wedding was certainly in the *extreme* of quietness; yet not so as to be in any way censured or remarked upon – and this was the order of the day.

The bridegroom came from Ashe Rectory where he had

hitherto lived with his brother, and Mr and Mrs Lefroy came with him, and another brother, Mr Edward Lefroy. Anne Lefroy, the eldest little girl, was one of the brides-maids, and I was the other. My brother had come from Winchester that morning, but was to stay only a few hours. We in the house had a slight early breakfast up stairs; and between 9 and 10 the bride, my mother, Mrs Lefroy, Anne and myself, were taken to church in our carriage. All the gentlemen walked. The weather was dull and cloudy, but it did not actually rain. The season of the year, the unfrequented road of half a mile to the lonely old church, the grey light within of a November morning making its way through the narrow windows, no stove to give warmth, no flowers to give colour and brightness, no friends, high or low, to offer their good wishes, and so to claim some interest in the great event of the day – all these circumstances and deficiencies must, I think, have given a gloomy air to our wedding. Mr Lefroy read the service, my father gave his daughter away. The Clerk of course was there, altho' I do not particularly remember him; but I am quite sure there was no one else in the church, nor was anyone else asked to the breakfast, to which we sat down as soon as we got back. I do not think this idea of sadness struck me at the time; the bustle in the house, and all the preparations had excited me, and it seemed to me as a festivity from beginning to end. The breakfast was such as best breakfasts then were: some variety of bread, hot rolls, buttered toast, tongue or ham and eggs. The addition of chocolate at one end of the table, and the wedding cake in the middle, marked the speciality of the day. I and Anne Lefroy, nine and six years old, wore white frocks and had white ribband on our straw bonnets, which, I suppose, were new for the occasion. Soon after breakfast, the bride and bridegroom departed. They had a long day's journey before them, to Hendon; the other Lefroys went home; and in the afternoon my mother and I went to Chawton to stay at the Great House, then occupied by my uncle Captain Austen and his large family. My father stayed behind for a few days, and then joined us. The servants had cake and punch in the evening, and I think I remember that Mr Digweed walked down to keep him company. Such were the wedding festivities of Steventon in 1814![32]

40

From the difference of our ages, my sister's marriage did not bring me much advancement; all continued the same as before; and I was 'Miss Caroline' in the house, as long as we remained at Steventon. But I *was* promoted to the use of a horse, and began to ride regularly. Our stable establishment consisted of three horses – two of them could carry a lady – they were useful animals, and were expected to take their turn as hunters besides. My father kept one horse in exercise; if he did not hunt, he rode. I think very few days passed all through the year, that he was not on horseback. But in the winter, two of them had to be exercised daily, and I was delighted to get often an hour's ride, with the groom, in a large meadow near the house. It was not safe, and I wonder now that it was allowed; but, it was said of the family, in after years, that they never thought any horse or pony could do wrong, and I suppose this confidence prevailed at Steventon. Our horses were steady animals enough, but in the winter they were kept in good condition, and were exhilarated by finding themselves on turf. We always took a canter up one end of the meadow. The horses knew exactly when they were to begin it, and after a little time, *go* they would, and *I* could not have stopped mine, if I had wished it, and the canter broke into a gallop. I suppose the groom was able to manage his steed, and we usually made the circuit very steadily, till we came to the cantering ground again, and then off the horses went at their own pleasure. I enjoyed it and was not frightened, till one day they both resolved to go home at a galloping pace. The shortest way to their stable was over a hedge and bank; so, neglecting the wide gap made on purpose for their use in going from one meadow to the other, the servant's horse, which was first, charged the fence – the man was as much run away with as I was. As his horse cleared the hedge *he* tumbled off behind, and fell exactly in front of mine, which was following with great energy. The surprise checked him, and I was able to manage him, till the man could come to my help. He *said* he threw himself off on purpose, because he thought it was the best way of stopping my horse. The hedge and bank were not very high, and I think that I should probably have got over safe – but I was frightened. My attendant then was not the groom, but a former servant who had come as a temporary help – a most steady trustworthy man, but no horseman. I do not remember whether I went exercising again, but as a practice it was given up. I rode though very often with my father and my brother, and I think riding was my greatest pleasure.

1815

In January Mrs Hinxman died. She was my mother's aunt, the Miss Craven who had disobliged her family by marrying their near neighbour, Mr Hinxman of Sennington in Gloucestershire. Years afterwards, the Craven relations benefited by this connection. One son remained to succeed his father at Sennington. He had no children, and he left his money, after his wife's death, amongst them. Fulwar and Charles Craven and Lady Pollen, Lady Austen, Mr and Mrs Fowle and Mrs Austen – the seven surviving cousins – got about £1,500 each, and most unexpectedly.

February 4th   Mary Bishop died, my mother's first cousin. She and her mother, who had been also a Miss Craven, lived at Fairford in Gloucestershire. They had fallen into deep poverty, and were helped a little by their relations.

February 20th   Mr Dennis, while dining at Mr Harwood's was seized with apoplexy and died the following morning. This brings before me again circumstances which whilst they were passing interested me greatly. If I am to write my own recollections the affairs of our neighbours must take their place in the story. With some few – the Harwoods especially – we were so intimately associated that my mother seemed to take part in all their troubles. Of their prosperities there were none that I can remember, and as tragedies make the deepest impression, I have no doubt that I thought much more about our old neighbours than I should have thought, had all been less unfortunate. I heard all, or nearly all, as it occurred. The kindness of the Deane family was much dwelt on by my father and mother; and also, a *little,* their singular unluckiness in having had such a trouble brought to their house; and now, in looking back and remembering, I do feel that Mr Harwood, in his support of the poor Dennises all

42

James–Edward
Austen, *ca.* 1828.

Miss Emma Smith,
ca. 1828.

Old cottages at Steventon.
(A nineteenth-century drawing, probably by Julia Lefroy.)

through their distress, did come up to any ideal which may have since been sketched of 'A Christian Gentleman'. It must be remembered that he had found himself a ruined man on his father's death about two years previously; to save, therefore, must be his constant daily object, so that the debts might be a little lessened every year. He now calculated that by the strictest economy throughout his whole life, he might leave the estate nearly clear at last for his nephew, then a young child; and this state of things must be borne in mind if, in the retrospect which I am now making, his bounty towards his distressed neighbour is to be rightly estimated.

Mr Dennis had lately come to the curacy of Overton. Very little was known about him, except that he had a large and still increasing family, and that he was poor; but how *very* poor, I suppose nobody suspected. Mr Harwood, amongst other old-world feelings, had *this* very strongly, that it was always a clergyman's duty to welcome into the neighbourhood any brother clergyman, be he rector or curate, if he knew of nothing against him; and so he lost no time in making Mr Dennis's acquaintance, and in asking him to come over, to share the family dinner, for all idea of any other sort of dinner company at Deane, was quite laid aside. Mr Dennis came – and whilst sitting at table, was seized with apoplexy and was carried upstairs senseless. Mr Lyford was sent for from Basingstoke and Mrs Dennis was summoned as soon as possible. She came with her eldest daughter and saw her husband breathe his last the following morning. Now that all was over, Mr Harwood, conjecturing *something* of the extreme family poverty, insisted that the funeral should take place from his house, and in order that the poor widow should not be forced away from her husband's remains, *she* was pressed to stay on, at the evident risk of what *might* and what actually *did* happen. She was expecting her confinement shortly and under the circumstances it was not wonderful she should have been suddenly taken ill, the night before the funeral, and that so her child came into the world at Deane.

Mr Dennis was buried on Thursday. My mother, who was always with the Harwoods on any emergency, spent the greater part of Wednesday and Thursday at Deane with them, and she took me with her – I suppose, for I could not have been much wanted, because there was nobody to leave me with at home, my father, I see, being just then at Chawton. I well remember sitting in the little front room upstairs, and watching the procession as it seemed slowly to glide from the house to the church. It was quite a plain funeral, but yet the grandest *I* had ever seen. Of the Dennis family there was the eldest daughter, just grown up, and several other sons and daughters of various ages. All were in deep and proper mourning, of which one particular still lingers in my memory, not as the mere shreds of an old dress, but as slightly characteristic. How Mr Harwood gave it all, the ladies of the family arranging it. The younger children were supplied with what was strong and plain and durable, so good black stuff was got for them. In those days the only materials used for deep mourning were stuff and bombasine. They were considered equally *deep*, but the latter was much finer and more expensive. For Mrs Dennis this was provided, with crape and all other accompaniments fit for a widow, and a bombasine gown also for the eldest daughter, who was with her in the house. But when Miss Dennis knew of it, she begged her next sister might have it instead, and *she* would take the stuff, for the second girl was at school, and she would like her to have the best; and so it was settled. I have been surprised to see how short a time elapsed between the death and the funeral – only three days – and I cannot but wonder *how* the mourning was got ready. I suppose all in the house, including my mother, helped to make it.[33]

Mrs Dennis remained at Deane the full time that could be thought necessary for her recovery, and was most carefully attended to. It was surmised she had never known so much comfort before, and it was quite certain she could not have had it in her home at Overton. Nothing was spared for her. Tho' poverty was in the house, she, the guest, was not to feel it. One day there was a question about wine. A little had been used at the funeral, and a very few bottles of white wine were all that remained of the old store; wine was never thought of now in the family except on very particular occasions. Mrs Anna Harwood made the not unreasonable suggestion that beer caudle should be sent up to Mrs

44

Dennis; it was equally wholesome and some people preferred it. But the master of the house was in the room, and when he comprehended what the ladies were talking about he positively ordered that as long as there was a drop remaining Mrs Dennis should have wine in her gruel. My mother, who had been present, mentioned this to a mutual friend and before long a small hamper of white wine found its way anonymously to Deane. Mr Harwood though was but ill-pleased – and it was some time before he quite forgave my mother, whom he rightly suspected of having been the reporter of this scarcity in his cellar.

To finish the tale of the Dennises I will now say that a very large subscription was raised for them by Mr Harwood's exertions amongst his friends, and that the family were in a manner provided for, as besides money the boys got nominations to charitable schools. The mother and the younger children were settled in a cottage at Overton, a real cottage, not much above a labourer's – I remember it well – and in time I believe all the young people were able to earn their own bread. One son became a clergyman, and one a doctor. Others took more humble positions but *generally* they turned out well, and I believe they were not ungrateful to Mr Harwood, who managed for them the sum that had been collected, and made himself a sort of guardian to the children; and once a year, for some time, all who were at Overton came to spend a day at Deane. I do not think that there ever turned up any relation of the Dennises willing or able to assist them. I often heard it said at home, 'How few would have done what Mr Harwood did for them!' He was very much honoured for it at our house, and most justly. It would not have been unreasonable that the actual funeral expenses should have been paid out of the very large subscription afterwards raised, but this, Mr Harwood would not hear of. Tho' every £50 expended placed at a farther distance the great object for which he now lived yet his notions of what hospitality and charity demanded remained the same. This misfortune of his neighbours had been in God's Providence brought to *him*. Lazarus had been laid at *his* door, and he must not be put away without such relief as the poor man's table could supply. The family had no claim upon him from

45

friendship or old acquaintanceship. They had come into the neighbourhood unknown and poor, and then the widow and children were suddenly left altogether destitute. 'I was a stranger and ye took me in' are all the words that need be added to this quite true tale.

In the May of this year I had an illness such as was then called bilious fever. Soon after I recovered, we went to spend a week at Eversley. Mr Debary was the clergyman there, and his sisters lived with him.[34] The place seemed to me beautiful – a running stream of water in the garden, and foxgloves, which I had never seen before, growing on the banks when we got out into the heath. The Sunday which we passed there, and it was a very hot one, was the 18th June – the decisive day of the battle of Waterloo. I do not remember how soon afterwards it was, that the news of the victory reached England.

October 24th   There came a letter to announce my Uncle Henry's serious and dangerous illness. He had then a house in Hans Place. Aunt Jane who was staying with him wished my father to come up, and so he and my mother rode that day to Chawton, and on the day following, he and Aunt Cassandra went to London, my mother remaining behind at Chawton, with Mrs Austen. My Aunt Martha was away in Berkshire, visiting various friends, and so my mother engaged to stay in the place of the daughters. It had been ruled in the family that Mrs Austen was never to be left alone – why, I do not know, for I am sure she was at that time, and long afterwards, perfectly well able to take care of herself, and she was as free from nervous fancies, as any creature that ever breathed. But the rule, whoever might have made it, was scrupulously observed. I was left at home to receive William Fowle who was coming for shooting. He stayed and shot the next day, and on the day following Mr Digweed received him as *his* guest. Then the Harwoods took me in for two nights and on Saturday I rode to Chawton, and there remained at my grandmother's. Captain Austen was also there.

My uncle's illness was low fever, and for several days they thought him dying; but a favourable turn came, and my father went home at the end of a week, but both my aunts

46

remained in Hans Place, and we stayed with my grand-mother about a month. Cassy Austen was also in the house. My father came over occasionally for a day or two. I quite remember it all, but I was not aware that our visit had lasted so long. I see my mother was away from her home just a month. During that time another child of Captain Austen's was born at the Great House – Herbert.[35]

At Christmas this year I made my first independent visit. It was to The Vine, for two whole days.

1816

On 18th January there is entered: 'Thanksgiving day for the Battle of Waterloo'.

February 20th   Captain Charles Austen's ship the *Phoenix* was lost. She went down – all the crew saved. The place is not noted; I do not remember where it was.[36] The pilot was on board. The *Phoenix had* been a lucky ship, Admiral Halsted having made his fortune in her, but her luck had now run out; perhaps she was not as seaworthy as she had been, tho' I do not recollect that this was ever said. No blame fell on the Captain, yet such a misfortune is always a disparagement; and the war being over, he knew he was likely to wait long for another ship.

Early in this year, I went with my mother to stay at Mrs Craven's and at Mr Fowle's – absent about three weeks. I notice that gradually less and less did my father make any visits. He had long ceased to dine out, and even the quiet family dinner at The Vine, on Sunday or any chance day in the week, is never noted now. He still went frequently to Chawton for one or two nights, but scarcely ever anywhere else.

This was a bad year for our family. The second and most serious misfortune was my Uncle Henry's bankruptcy, announced on 16th March, an entire surprise at our house, and as little foreseen I believe by the rest of the family. But the apprehension of the coming evil had had much to do with his own illness a few months previously. The Bank was in Henrietta Street, Covent Garden – Austen, Maunde & Tilson. They had connected themselves with the Alton bank,

47

which had failed, and I suppose *this* hastened the crisis. I know none of the particulars as to the cause of this ruin. My uncle had been living for some years past at considerable expense, but not more than might become the head of a flourishing bank, and no blame of personal extravagance was ever imputed to him. He had not long before been appointed Receiver General for Oxfordshire, for which a suretyship of £30,000 had been required. This sum the two sureties had to pay – Mr Leigh Perrot £10,000, Mr Knight £20,000. My father and Captain Austen some hundreds, on account of an Army Agency, for which *they* had bound themselves, besides what small sums were standing in the bank; so that altogether this blow fell heavily on the family.

To my uncle himself it was ruin, and he saw the world before him, to begin again. In about a fortnight he came to Steventon, *apparently*, for truly it could *not* have been, in unbroken spirits. I believe he had even then decided on taking Orders. He *had* been destined for the Church, but had preferred going into business and had left St John's College early. He was a Fellow there. Now the old learning was to be looked up, and he went to Oxford to see about taking the necessary degree.[37] He had very good abilities, and such as were always ready for use; fond of all sorts of reading, I do not suppose that books had ever been entirely laid aside during the business years of his life, and examinations were not overstrict in the year 1816, so that altogether no difficulties opposed his entrance into the profession to which he now turned with all the energy of a sanguine elastic nature. He was I see many times at Steventon during this year, and then it was, I suppose, that I got to like him so very much, as I remember but little of him previously.

In May my two aunts went to Cheltenham.[38] They took Steventon in their way, to leave my cousin Cassy with us. They stayed about three weeks and then took her back. My mother was very unwell [for a] great part of this summer, and in August she was advised to go to Cheltenham. Aunt Cassandra accompanied us, and we stopped one night at Kintbury, to take up Mary Jane Fowle. We stayed three weeks, left Mary Jane at her home, and got to Steventon; my aunt took me on with her to spend two or three weeks at Chawton.

On 19th December my Uncle Henry went from Steventon to Winchester for his examination, and on the following day proceeded to Salisbury where he was ordained to the curacy of [Chawton].

This December my brother left school for good. My father had an accident out riding and broke the small bone of his leg. He kept on the sofa for some time and taught me chess.

1817

My brother was now entered at Oxford, at Exeter College, and a Craven Scholarship falling vacant, it seemed as if it must be his by natural right – there was no other Founder's Kin to dispute it with him.[39] Some certificates of marriages and baptisms were required, and he went to Bishopston to obtain them. On a former occasion, when William Fowle had claimed one of these Exhibitions, it had been thought advisable to get the baptismal certificate of his grand-mother, Jane Craven, to prove that she was her father's daughter, but it could never be discovered where any of Governor Charles Craven's children *had* been baptised. He was known to have had a place in Worcestershire – Lenchwick – but the register there gave no information. Enquiry was made at other places, considered possible, but equally in vain; and some of the family professed to believe, that Mrs Craven, having been a very bad mother, had never had her children christened at all.

The missing link in the pedigree had never, as yet, occasioned much inconvenience. The authorities had been satisfied without it, but now they were stricter in their demands; for the spirit of reform had crept in, and they wished to be able to throw open the Scholarship to competition, as they were enjoined to do, if no Founder's Kin should claim it, therefore they insisted that the candidate should prove his descent and give legal assurance that the late Mrs Lloyd from whom he claimed, was the daughter of the Honble Charles Craven. But a few days remained when my mother bethought her of getting affidavits to this effect from Mrs Criswick, formerly a servant in Governor

Craven's family, and Mrs Hulbert, an old friend who had known them all intimately. This was done, and the attestation reached the Vice Chancellor's hands in time, but only just in time, to secure to my brother, the £25 per annum for 14 years which perhaps in the days of John Lord Craven of Ryton, Salop, was a decent maintenance for an Oxford scholar.

The registry of Governor Craven's children was found long years afterwards by my brother, whilst on a visit to the Seymours of Kinwarton. It was in the little church of Norton, close to Lenchwick, that they had been christened – several of them – my grandmother and Mrs Fowle were amongst them.[40]

On Friday 28th March Mr Leigh Perrot died. My father, whom he had left his executor, was summoned to Scarlets by a letter Sunday morning, and he and my mother set off immediately after service. On 5th April, Mr Leigh Perrot was buried in Wargrave churchyard. On the 19th my father and mother came home.[41] In June and July she spent much time at Winchester, in attendance on Aunt Jane, who died there on the morning of 18th July, at half past four. She was buried on the 24th in Winchester Cathedral.[42]

On 30th August I went to school at the Miss Burneys, Kingsgate Street, Winchester.

In September my father had a serious attack of illness, and from that period I date his rapid decline. He never recovered to even the very poor state of health which had been his portion through many previous years, for as long as my memory could go back. But he did get better, and in October went to Worthing for change of air. I saw him at Winchester where a family party gathered. Aunt Cassandra joined them to go on to Worthing, and Mrs B. Lefroy [Anna] came from Wyards at the same time, just to see her father, as also, I think, my aunt Miss Lloyd. They made but a short stay at Worthing; the air was not beneficial, and my father and mother spent a week at Chawton and then returned home.

1818

March 1st 'Mr Cookson began doing duty at Sherborne

[St John]'. This, I believe, my father never attempted to do, after his illness of the preceding year. Mr Cookson's assistance was but for a short time. He was the curate of Deane.

The entries all through this summer are of the usual friends coming and going. In July, I came home for the holidays. On 22nd of that month, Mr Maxwell of Ewshott died. His death made a great change in the fortunes of our neighbours, the Lefroys of Ashe. They took possession of Ewshott [Itchel Manor] and from this time resided there for several months every year.

July 31st My brother joined Mrs Heathcote and her son and Miss Bigg, in a tour through Wales. All this time my poor father was gradually getting worse, his malady increasing and his strength failing. He determined once more to try change of air, and to give himself what *would* have been a great pleasure in better days, the indulgence of a tour down the Wye. He had a delight in natural scenery, and pleased himself with the idea of following Gilpin's footsteps along the banks of that 'Gentle River'.[43] He was interested in making all the arrangements for our tour but as the time approached for our starting, he felt it would be too much for him and the plan was altered – we were not to go so far as to reach the Wye, and we were to be away only a week; and we fell short even of *this* – but we *did* set off, my father and mother and myself. We made Chawton the beginning of our tour, *he* thinking it right that if well enough to go out anywhere, he should go and see his mother. His attention to her, during all my recollection, was great, especially so, considering that it was always an effort to him to leave his own home. Not many months ever passed without his riding over to Chawton, and he gave up this habit very unwillingly. I *can* remember latterly his setting off once or twice to go there, and turning back after a few miles because he felt unequal to going on.

We now stayed one night at my grandmother's, and it was the last time that the mother and son ever met. The next day we went on to Southampton, stayed there some hours, and at the close of a lovely summer's evening, got to Lyndhurst, where we slept. At the inn we found the servant and two horses from Steventon, as had been arranged, my father

51

hoping to ride through the New Forest – the only way in which he could really have enjoyed it, for the inside of a carriage was at all times hateful to him. But he found he was not strong enough for this. If he made the attempt, of which I am not certain, he rode but a little way and the horses were useless. We stopped at Rufus's Stone, and lingered some time near it. We had a beautiful drive through the Forest; our point was Amesbury, where we slept. On our road thither from Salisbury we saw Stonehenge. Further progress had been planned, to see Longleat, and some other places; but at the end of this, our third day's *movement* – travelling it could scarcely be called – my father found himself only the worse for what he was doing and was anxious to get home again. So the next morning we turned back, and stopped a little while at Salisbury. I think the Music Meeting was going on there. There was, at any rate, some great gathering, and we found amongst the number William Fowle, the vicar of Amesbury. We had just missed him at his own place and had inspected, without his presence, the church and his vicarage. Now he did the honours of Salisbury, and went with us into the Cathedral. Afterwards we took the straight road home and got to Steventon by dinner time.

The following week I went back to school. My father made a few notes on what we had seen. I will transcribe, not his notes, but the reflexion with which they were wound up. He says, ' "We travel", Gilpin observes, "for various purposes", and he enumerates several; but none, if I remember them right, was exactly *my* purpose. I travelled to get health, i.e., in the rational expectation that the woods and heaths of the New Forest would brace relaxed nerves, and the action of a post-chaise rectify a disordered stomach. I had however some better motive to direct my route and determine my time. I went *where* I did to see my mother, whom I had never visited since my long illness, and I went *when* I did, that I might have my Caroline's company. In the pleasure I expected from these circumstances, I have felt no disappointment'.

December 23rd   I came home, and left school for good.

1819

This summer it was suggested and much advised by all friends, that my father should go to London for medical advice, and at length he resolved on doing so. I think it was but a ceremonial observance on all sides, and that neither he himself, nor his family who urged it, had any real hope of benefit from the measure. Dr Southey was the physician fixed on, I really believe because he was the brother of Robert Southey, and the nephew of Dr Hill then staying in the neighbourhood and from whom my father bore a letter of introduction.[44] I accompanied my father and mother to London. We slept at Bagshot and the next day, June 28th, we finished our journey, and early enough to be in lodgings before night. We were in No. [107] Great Russell Street in large and handsome apartments. The place had long been out of fashion, and the houses which had been built for wealthy occupants, were let out in lodgings. There was a large entrance hall, with a painted ceiling and a wide staircase. The largest drawing-room looked into a small garden.[45] Aunt Cassandra joined us in London, for she also needed medical advice, and my brother for part of the time.

Dr Southey came, and was in regular attendance, and at first he gave encouragement, or was *supposed* to do so. His manners were very pleasant, and no doubt he said the best he *could* say. His visits I think were agreeable to the patient. We stayed in London a fortnight – it seemed a short time considering the purpose for which we came – but my father longed to be at home again, and Dr Southey did not urge any further stay. He must have seen he could do no good – so we departed. The horses had been brought up, for it was only by riding that my father could get much air and exercise. His dislike to a carriage I have mentioned. He did, I think, ride several times, attended by his groom, for it was no longer safe that he should ride alone. And I cannot mention this servant, William Alexander, without adding a few words of praise and gratitude for his faithful attendance on my father during the last few months of his life. He was a very young man but he had been with us two or three years, and he had attached himself so strongly to his master, that all he did for

53

him seemed a labour of love. Up to the last, William assiduously attended on him with a patience and affection that knew no weariness.

We were to go down by the other road, and take Scarlets in our way. My father, always desiring the open air, and horse exercise, persuaded himself that he could ride down. He set off before us with his servant, we three ladies had the carriage, my brother was to follow by coach. But at Cranford Bridge we found he had halted, unable to proceed further on horseback, and obliged to take my place in the carriage. I was put outside the coach which soon came by, with my brother on it, and a very delightful way of travelling I thought it was. The coach was very full and I could only be taken by good-nature on the box, between the coachman and a gentleman – they were very careful of me – and in this manner I made my first approach to Scarlets.[46]

The coach put us down at the entrance to the lane, and my brother and I walked up to the house, and had to introduce ourselves to its mistress, whom *I* had never seen before, nor he, since the days of his early childhood. It was a beautiful summer's evening and some times I can recall *how* it all looked. Under shady trees and through green grass, a spotless carriage road of fine gravel stretched itself along, without much meandering, to the hall door of the red brick house; and this hall door was curiously set in a white wooden projection, such as I cannot describe. We all thought it unsightly outside; but within, it helped to shape out as pretty an entrance hall on a small scale as I have ever seen. We were very well amused at Scarlets, going about the gardens and shrubbery, and looking at many things that were shown us in the house. We stayed ten whole days and then got home again.

My father grew worse almost daily, getting by degrees to take his meals in his own room, and living very much apart. Yet I think we had even more guests than usual in the house. Amongst them was a drawing-master who stayed with us for a week. My father whilst in London had made this arrangement with a young man, a Mr Sergeant. It was intended chiefly for *my* benefit, but he himself took great pleasure in the drawing lessons. He was no longer equal to much exercise, and he was glad of an indoors occupation. He had great natural taste for drawing, and he had practised it a little in his youth, but *I* had scarcely ever before seen him with a pencil in his hand. *Now* he took it up again, with the help of the young artist, who was very obliging with advice and assistance; and from this time he continued so to amuse himself, chiefly with indian ink sketches as long as he was able to hold the brush. Soon it came that his head would not bear the motion of *any* carriage (he had gone out in a phaeton, which a good neighbour had lent for his accommodation). Now his craving for 'out of doors' could only be gratified by sitting out in a bath-chair, almost daily for several hours during the autumn, in one particular spot, sunny and sheltered. I suppose everyone knew he was failing fast, for I see how all his family and my mother's came for a few days one after another about this time. On 20th October Mr Bellas took the curacy of Sherborne [St John] and Mr Davis living at Deane engaged for Steventon; my father was no longer able even to get to church.

The end of the autumn was a sad season. Our friends had come and gone, nor could guests have been any longer received in the house. One of my uncles, Henry or Charles, came sometimes for a night from Chawton, and I used anxiously to hope for their arrival. My mother was more than once laid up with severe bilious attacks, brought on no doubt by long-continued anxieties. I was scarcely more than a child, and our chief dependence was on William Alexander. The weather became too cold for sitting out but to breathe the open air was still my father's great desire, and William contrived for him a sort of litter, so that with the help of another man he could be borne along in an armchair, and this expedient was practised for a little while longer. He still occupied himself with drawing and more chiefly in composition. He had engaged in a long poem – somewhat after the manner of Cowper – and he continued to write whilst he was yet able to keep up. Mr Davis frequently came to sit with him and these visits gave him pleasure. On 17th November he became worse, and never left his bed afterwards; I think he was more comfortable *so;* and tho' he had made up his mind that *there* he must always remain, he did not at first expect that the end would so soon follow. His mind continued active as before. He put into verse three of the Psalms, dictating them, and wrote several letters in the same way. His daughter Mrs Lefroy came again to see him; she had been with us in September.

It was about a week before his death that he became aware he was sinking fast. My brother came from Oxford. On 13th December 1819 my father breathed his last, at half-past eleven at night. On Saturday the 18th he was buried in Steventon churchyard; the grave being made on the spot he had long before chosen for his last resting-place. The funeral was attended by my brother and our four uncles. Captain Charles Austen remained with us for a few days, the others went back to Chawton. After Christmas we paid a short visit to my grandmother.

1820

Our time at Steventon soon drew to a close. The living was at once given to my Uncle Henry but only in *trust,* to hold for his nephew William Knight, for about three years. Whilst we remained, he served the church, coming over weekly from Chawton, which of course was inconvenient - and besides he quickly secured two or three pupils, and it was necessary he should have a house to receive them in. The dates of the next few weeks do not appear, but I think we were out by the end of January. A deluge seemed to come to drive us away. It was an unusually severe winter, and much snow fell. A thaw came on suddenly and one night we were roused by a rush of water pouring into the cellars, with the noise of a cataract, and on going down the men found all the ground floor under water. There were drains made on purpose to meet such occurrences, but nobody had thought about them, and so high was the water round the house, that the men punted themselves out in a tub, to reach the places they had to open. Next morning the cellar looked like the scene of a shipwreck – all the barrels displaced, some floating and some sunk. The water drained off in time, but the hall and the two parlours retained so much dampness that we never lived downstairs again, and had all our meals brought up to the study. I think this happened about a week before we went away. My brother was the first to go; he had to return to Oxford. In a few days afterwards, my mother and I departed, setting off about 9 o'clock to make the day's journey to Bath.

We left Uncle Henry in possession. He seemed to have renewed his youth, *if* indeed he could be said ever to have lost it, in the prospect before him. A fresh life was in view - he was eager for work – eager for pupils – was sure very good ones would offer – and to hear him discourse you would have supposed he knew of no employment so pleasant and honourable, as the care and tuition of troublesome young men. He was also looking forward secretly to his own marriage; it took place in the following [April].[47] This we did not know of as certain, but his intention had been guessed in the family for some time. He was always very affectionate in manner to us, and paid my mother every due attention, but his own spirits he could *not* repress, and it is not pleasant to *witness* the elation of your successor in gaining what *you* have lost; and altogether tho' we left our home with sad hearts, we did not desire to linger in it any longer. My mother's old friend, Mrs Hulbert, received us at Bath. She had just lost her only sister, for whom she very sincerely mourned, and she offered us a *quiet* retreat for a little while. We travelled all day and got in between five and six – 32 Gay Street. The city of Bath by lamplight, as we approached, was a beautiful sight.

The chapter of Steventon is closed; but when I first thought of reviving my own life-long recollections by the aid of the old pocket-books, I intended to follow their guidance into the other homes with very different surroundings. Now I find this cannot be; I could not any longer make out a simple narrative of one family household, with notices here and there of a few old friends who had always been near neighbours, and as such, had made a part of our world. Afterwards we found new friends and made various intimacies, and when I look back upon the employments, and the interests, and the changes of our life, I find it would be impossible to follow one straight road of narrative. Little paths break out in all directions, most of them leading nowhere, but they are distractions, and the clue is lost amongst them. The many, with whom we became from time to time intimately associated, would come up a confused throng, such as I could not reduce to any order. Some few things I would have said, and thought to say, but to separate them intelligibly from the mere gossip, from the dust and rubbish with which they are mixed up, I see now to be impossible. The attempt would bewilder me too much.

I shall therefore, if I continue my researches, mark only dates, noting down in due order the time during which we occupied different houses, and noticing the principal family events, so as to form a table of reference if it should ever be required.

At Frog Firle, July 20th 1873

1820

December 4th   Mrs Hulbert, who went as usual to spend the winter at Bath, left us in possession of her house at Speen.
December 30th   Miss Murden died at Hungerford.[48]

1821

June 30th   We left Mrs Hulbert's house for one which my mother rented of Miss Vincent in the Donnington Road, a little way out of Speenhamland, my mother, my brother and myself keeping together.
December 15th   Mr Thomas Leigh buried at Monk Sherborne. He was the imbecile brother of my grandmother and of Mr Leigh Perrot. He had been placed at Monk Sherborne years before, under the care of the Culhams of that parish.[49]

1822

January 23rd   Mrs Bramston died at Oakley Hall; on the 31st, buried at Deane.

Emma and
James-Edward
Austen-Leigh, 1870.

Caroline in later life.

1823

March 26th   Our house at Speen broken into between five and six in the evening. Many articles stolen. We were at Kintbury, the maids had gone out.

June 1st   My brother was ordained in London by the Bishop of Winchester, to the curacy of Newtown, Hants. He did duty the following Sunday at Kintbury.

July 15th   Mrs F. Austen died at Government House, Gosport, a few days after the birth of her eleventh child.

1825

May 25th   We took possession of Mr Arbuthnot's house at Newtown which my mother rented of him at £20 per annum.

1827

My grandmother Mrs Austen died at her home at Chawton, January 18th, ten minutes before two in the morning, aged 87 the September before; she was buried at Chawton on the 23rd.

1828

December 10th   Our domestic party broke up, never to be re-united. I accompanied my brother to Tring Park, and in Tring church on the 16th he was married to Miss Emma Smith.[50]

December 21st   Mr John Hinxman died at Sennington, and left his money, after the decease of his wife, amongst his maternal cousins – Mr and Mrs Fowle, Mrs Austen, Mrs F. Austen, Lady Pollen, Fulwar and Charles Craven, Esq.[51]

1829

August 27th   The Revd Benjamin Lefroy died at Ashe, ten minutes after twelve, that is the 28th; he was buried in the family vault within the church, September 3rd. I was at Ashe.

September 26th   My brother's first child – a boy – born at Tring Park.

November 6th   Cholmeley christened. Sponsors Mrs Leigh Perrot, Sir Charles Smith, and Mrs Knight. Only Sir Charles Smith present.[52]

November 13th   Mrs B. Lefroy left Ashe and went to live at West Ham with her brother-in-law, Mr Edward Lefroy.[53]

1830

November 17th   'The country in a disturbed state from the rising of the labourers'. We had a little mob at Newtown of fourteen people. They were easily dispersed, and were very civil.

Sunday 21st   'A meeting after Church in our room, for the good of the country, where nothing was settled'. This same Sunday evening, Mr Fowle, in fear of the mob which was gathering in great force at Kintbury, sent away Mrs Fowle, his daughters and granddaughter, and they took with them their neighbour Miss Smith of Fosbury. Some of the party went to Mrs Craven's at Speen and some to Mr Best's in Newbury. My uncle kept the house, with his son Charles. They were threatened, but the Vicarage was not attempted, and after a while the people dispersed.

22nd   'The country in great confusion.'

23rd   'The confusion still greater.' The mob did not come up to our house, but they went to Adbury and broke the threshing machines of Sir James Fellowes and of Mr Villebois.

24th   'The rioters at Inkpen and Kintbury were taken and carried to Newbury.'[54]

December 20th   'The trial of Hampshire rioters went on at Winchester.'

December 28th   'Sir James Fellowes' wood-house set on fire.' The trials ended at Winchester – several to be hung. These riotings, which were very general in the eastern and southern counties, were amongst the agricultural labourers. They were instigated and encouraged, as was supposed, by men of a higher class, and of more intelligence, but their promptings were given in secret, and they kept aloof from all dangers. The poor labourers *were* very badly off; wages were very low and work itself was scarce. Threshing with the flail had always been one of their most profitable employments, and this was being gradually withdrawn from them by the use of threshing machines (horse power). They were led to believe that the farmers might be terrified into giving up the machines; the first step must be to break them all to pieces, and this they employed themselves in doing for the two or three days. After breaking the machines they demanded money, and unfortunately for themselves they usually got it. Sometimes they were paid to pass on. Each day the mobs got more violent in their language, but no injury was inflicted on any human being, nor ever contemplated by the labourers. In a very few days a detachment of soldiers came to our assistance and the rioters were as helpless and as passive as a flock of sheep. The magistrates secured some of the ringleaders – as many as they chose – and the rest dispersed. A Special Commission went its rounds to try the prisoners, and several were condemned to death. It seems impossible now to believe this. The capital offence was extorting money by intimidation. The men themselves, tho' they knew they were going against the law, had *no* idea they were running the risk of being hung. Three men were sentenced to death at Reading, all parishioners of Kintbury.

1831

January 10th   Mr Fowle went to Reading to visit the three condemned men, Winterborne, Oakley and Darling. He found them all three in the same cell – so placed perhaps in order to receive him. The warder asked if he should stay, and Mr Fowle said, no. The men were very humble and grateful to him. He had done all he could, by means of petitions, to get their lives spared, and this they knew. They were employing themselves in roasting some potatoes on the stove, in order as they said, to eat their last meal together. The interview was intensely painful to my uncle. The following morning was fixed for the executions, but at the last hour a reprieve came for two, and Winterborne suffered alone. His body was brought to Kintbury that same afternoon, and buried with the funeral service the following day. Many Kintbury men were transported, some for life, others for a term of years. I never heard that any came back, but we did learn that two of these prospered very well in their banishment – and probably so did many others also. The destiny of Norris and Bates fixed them in Van Diemen's Land [Tasmania]. They were a bricklayer and a carpenter, neither of them of very good repute at home, Norris an habitual drunkard. This propensity he entirely conquered, and refused to be paid for his work partly in drink – a custom that was very common in the place. They both saved money and lived in credit – and perhaps established respectable families in the Colony – but I am not able to trace them to their end.

1833

In March we joined the Edward Austens and went to Hastings for my brother's health. We remained until 21st May.
November 9th Mr and Mrs Edward Austen settled at Speen in Mrs Parry's house.

1836

April 5th We left Newtown (having occupied Mr Arbuthnot's house there for nearly 11 years) and came to Speen.
November 13th 'This morning at 20 minutes before 9, Mrs Leigh Perrot breathed her last, without a struggle.' In the house at Scarlets there had been for two or three days my mother, my brother, and Aunt Cassandra, summoned by Mr Taylor.
November 17th 'Sir William and Lady Welby came. Mrs Leigh Perrot's Will was opened, and found highly satisfactory to my dear Edward and I hope to every branch of *her* family.'[55]
November 18th Admiral and Captain Austen and Mr Henry Austen came.
November 19th The funeral took place at Wargrave. Besides the party in the house, it was attended by Mr John

62

Cholmeley and Mr Glascott, and Mr Taylor of Wargrave. There were three coaches and three carriages. All was over soon after twelve, and by two all were gone except Admiral and Captain Austen, who stayed and went to church the next day, Sunday. On Monday 21st they left Scarlets, as did also Miss C. Austen.

December 28th   Agreed to take ·Mrs Parry's house at Speen for one year.

'Thus ends the year 1836, an eventful one to us.'

1837

January 3rd   'Went up to Edward's to see them before they left Speen. They went to Scarlets as their future home. God grant they may have health long to enjoy it.'

January 10th   'I commenced being Mr Allen's tenant at Speen at £140 a year.'

February 4th   'Edward this day took the name of Leigh to that of Austen.'

March 3rd   'Admiral Austen a K.C.B., we saw it in the newspaper.'

1839

March 31st   Mrs Craven died in London and on Friday 5th April she was buried at Sennington in Gloucestershire.

Sunday, 26th May   'My dear sister Eliza expired this morning, soon after 9 o'clock.'

December 5th   The postage of letters altered to 4d. each all over the United Kingdom.

1840

January 5th   The penny post began this day all over the kingdom and the 4d. postage ceased which had taken place December 5th 1839.

March 9th   'At 20 minutes past 7 this morning, Mr Fowle breathed his last.'

December 31st   'This year, like the last, has given me much to lament and to be sorry for. It has taken from me three in whom I felt great interest – my brother-in-law the Revd Fulwar Craven Fowle, my old friend Mrs Hulbert, and my valued friend Mrs Villebois – but it has also given me much to be thankful for, in my own, my son and daughter's good health, and in the health of his wife and eight children.'

1842

July 27th   Mrs Chute died at The Vine, ten minutes before twelve at night. Edward was sent for and was with her when she breathed her last.

1843

January 26th, Thursday   'Heard this morning from Sir Francis Austen of my sister's death. Cassandra, his sister, went to him on Monday evening.'
January 31st   'The remains of my departed sister Martha, Lady Austen, were interred on the north side of Wymering churchyard, Hants – attended only by her husband Sir Francis, and his two eldest sons, Frank and Henry.'
August 1st   'I walked to Newbury, called on Mrs Bunbury and Mrs Michell, and on Mrs R. Best. We drank tea at Miss Seymour's – met the usual village party.'

This is the last entry. On the day following, August 2nd, after returning from a drive to Sandleford, my mother was seized with paralysis. She died the day following, August 3rd, 24 hours after the seizure.

Continued from my own diaries.
August 11th   We followed my mother to her grave in Steventon churchyard.

I remained on at Speen, not being able to get a tenant for Mr Allen's house for the remainder of the lease. It was not till the summer of 1844 that I was able to leave it. On 10th July I left Speen, going first to Aunt Cassandra's at Chawton – which place I have never seen since. I did not settle anywhere, but visited various relations and friends, making my headquarters at Scarlets.

1845

On the first of February I left my brother's house, and took possession of my own at Knowl Hill, renting it at £55 per annum of Mr Curtis. I had two meadows besides garden ground.

In March, on the 17th, being much alarmed by bad reports of Aunt Cassandra, I went off to Portsdown Lodge, where she was lying in the last stage of weakness. She had gone there as well as usual to take leave of her brother and his family, for Sir Francis was on the point of sailing in the *Vindictive,* to take his command on the West India Station. All the inmates had cleared out and were on board the vessel at Portsmouth when I got there. It was impossible for my uncle to delay his departure. He came over to see his sister once – that was all he could do. I found only Uncle Henry left in charge. My Uncle Charles joined us ere long. On the morning of Saturday 22nd Aunt Cassandra passed away at twenty minutes before four. Her illness had begun with some sort of seizure in the head, and she never rallied much, tho' her mind was not at all affected even up to the last. She was buried at Chawton on Friday 28th March. Her age was 72.

1851

I bought Wargrave Lodge of Frederic Johnson Esq; I gave £1,200 for the house and land. Fixtures afterwards of Mr Bode who was then the tenant, £35.

1852

November 19th   My uncle Edward Knight Esq, died this day at Godmersham Park – age 85. In this year died also my uncle Admiral Charles Austen on board the *Pluto* steamer on the Irrawaddy River, Burmah.

1853

April 28th   I dined at Scarlets for the last time with the

Austen-Leighs. On the following day April 29th my brother and sister with their family left the place, and began their residence at Bray, in the vicarage house. Scarlets was let to Mr Littledale. It was a very cold wet day.

October 14th   I took possession of Wargrave Lodge.

1857

July 25th   Louisa Lefroy was married at Monk Sherborne to the Revd Septimus Bellas, rector of that place.

1858

July 26th   I went to Southsea and took lodgings at Albert Villa, and was joined there in a day or two by Mrs Seymour Terry with her two youngest children and nurse. On 12th August we spent the day at Portsdown Lodge. The last time of my visiting that place, and my last interview with my uncle Sir Francis Austen.

1859

May 10th   Lizzie Lefroy married at Monk Sherborne to the Revd Arthur Loveday.

1860

June   Sold my three shares in the Portsmouth Floating Bridge for £75. They had been bought for £87 in 1838.[56]

December 4th   I left my house at Wargrave to join my two nephews Charles and Spencer Leigh in Sussex, at Frog Firle, a farm belonging to the Duke of Devonshire of about 550 acres, in the parish of Alfriston.

1863

October 9th   I left Frog Firle for the winter, my house at Wargrave being empty. I intended to make arrangements for letting it in the following spring, but on learning that Mr Nicholl was enquiring for a house in that parish I determined to offer it for sale, and he agreed to buy it.

1864

January 7th　Cholmeley was married in Westminster Abbey to Melesina Mary, eldest daughter of the Revd Richard Trench, late Dean of Westminster and newly appointed Archbishop of Dublin.

February 20th　I left my house. Spent a little time with Mrs [Anna] Lefroy, who had recently settled at Southern Hill near Reading, and on the 29th I came back to my nephews at Frog Firle.

1865

January 22nd　A son born to Cholmeley, at 39 Sussex Gardens.

August 10th　My uncle Sir Francis Austen, Admiral of the Fleet, died this day at his own house Portsdown Lodge. He was 91 last April. The last survivor of six brothers and two sisters – several of whom had lived to old age, but none so old as himself.

1871

April 27th　Burnt, as I had long intended to do, all that yet remained extant of my childish writings. Lines on the death of Farmer Hyde, the earliest, no date. Letter in verse to my brother at Winchester 1815. Comedy in verse the same year – imitated I suppose from Hayley's Comedies – one of which 'The Mausoleum' I knew very well. The last, my own comedy, I could not bring myself to read again. A few scraps besides, all in verse. On what I did read, I pass this judgement. That they showed wonderful facility in rhyme and measure for a child of ten years old, but that they were flippant, and in bad taste – an attempt at the comic, where comedy should not have been – and I wonder that they passed without rebuke.[57]

1872

May 30th   I went for a week to Reading. To Miss Hawkins, 1 Albion Place – in order to see my sister Mrs Lefroy who was very ill. I visited her every day – she kept chiefly upstairs on the sofa. On the first of the following September, she died at her house at Southern Hill, near Reading; 79, last April. She was buried at Ashe September 6th in the churchyard, near to [her daughter] Jemima's grave.

In October this year, the 29th, my brother came. On the 31st, coursing on the hill; the weather bad, cold and wet, but my brother kept out on foot nearly the whole day. On the morrow I drove him to join the shooters at the Foxcover, and left him there. He had luncheon with them and stayed till the end of the day walking back and he did not appear over-tired. This was his last visit to Frog Firle.

1874

April 14th   I went to Norwood, joining Mr and Mrs Austen-Leigh, Amy and Mary, who had come up for a few days to see the Crystal Palace. Spent that afternoon and many hours the next morning in the Palace, where we had luncheon. This was the last time I was ever to see my dear brother. He died on the 8th of the following September at Bray Vicarage in his 76th year. His illness was very short. He kept his room but a few days, and although his family, considering his age, were in some degree anxious about him, there was no real cause for alarm till the night before. He breathed his last about 10 o'clock Tuesday morning the 8th. He had suffered grievously for many years past from some sort of rheumatic affection and was not able to take much exercise; but he did keep about, often in a surprising manner, as when the year before he had followed the coursing for a whole day, at Frog Firle. His health was good for his time of life.

On Saturday the 14th, he was buried in Bray churchyard. His widow, his seven sons and two daughters and myself, followed him to his grave. Sir John Seymour, several nephews and many friends also attended him to the last. It was a lovely September day, and in the afternoon the lawn and the gay flowers and the sparkling river, looked only too bright and beautiful! They did not mourn for him – and he had loved them so well!

Notes

Jane Austen's letters are referred to by the numbers given them in R.W. Chapman (ed.) *Jane Austen's Letters* (Oxford University Press, 2nd edn 1964).

1   Unpublished letter from James Austen at Steventon to Mrs Leigh-Perrot at Scarlets, 8 April 1819.

2   W. and R.A. Austen-Leigh: *Jane Austen, her Life and Letters* (1913), p. 363.

3   M.A. Austen-Leigh: *James Edward Austen Leigh, a Memoir* (1911), pp. 48–9.

4   M.A. Austen-Leigh, *op.cit.*, p. 65.

5   M.A. Austen-Leigh, *op.cit.*, p. 137.

6   Caroline's own manuscript was published in full by the Jane Austen Society in 1952, entitled *My Aunt Jane Austen*.

7   Mrs Lloyd (1729–16 April 1805) is mentioned in several of Jane Austen's letters. No. 39 refers specifically to her loss of memory, and No. 43 to her imminent death.

8   Mrs Lefroy (*née* Anne Brydges, 1749–16 December 1804), was the wife of the Revd George Lefroy, rector of the neighbouring parish of Ashe. She was known locally as 'Madam Lefroy', and was Jane Austen's great friend and patron since the latter's childhood. She is mentioned often in Jane's earlier letters and in 1808, on the fourth anniversary of her death, Jane wrote a poem to her memory. In 1814 her youngest son Ben married Jane's niece Anna.

9   Mrs Stent (—— ?1812) was a friend of Mrs Lloyd's from the latter's Tewkesbury days. References in Jane Austen's letters suggest that she was a pathetic but tiresome old lady.

10   Caroline did not know the date of her great-grandfather Charles Craven's governorship of South Carolina, and indeed she seems to have been told very little about him. A brief investigation into his career, as given in the *Calendar of State Papers, Treasury Papers* and *Journal of the Commissioners for Trade and Plantations,* suggests that his immediate descendants may have preferred to forget about him as soon as possible.

Charles Craven (1682–1754) was the youngest brother of William, 2nd Lord Craven, who in 1708 was the Lord Palatine of the Province of Carolina, one of the newly-founded English colonies on the eastern seaboard of North America. No doubt due to his elder brother's influence, Charles was made the Secretary of South Carolina in 1709, and then appointed Governor in 1711. At first all went well; he was commended by the English Government in 1712 for his bravery in helping to defend North Carolina from Indian attacks, and received an increase in salary. He was commended again in 1715 for bravery during another Indian uprising.

However, Charles attempted to increase his private fortune in ways rather too openly dishonest, and reports of his malpractices travelled back across the Atlantic to government ears in London. Between 1714 and 1716 there were accusations that he was obstructing Customs officers in the execution of their duties so that illegal trade flourished. At the end of 1715 there began a lawsuit which was probably the cause of his ultimate downfall. A Spanish nobleman, the Marquis of Navarrez, who was then in Jamaica, arranged with an English sea-captain for himself and family, together with their effects to the value of £16,000, to be taken to the coast of Carthagena. The sea-captain robbed and marooned the unfortunate Spaniards, but was then forced by bad weather to seek shelter in the harbour of Charlestown, South Carolina, where he was arrested, the stolen goods recovered and handed to the Governor for safe-keeping. Charles Craven now yielded to temptation – he allowed the pirate to escape and retained the Marquis's goods, despite being ordered by the Government to hand them back when representations had been made in London by the Spanish Ambassador.

In 1716 Charles relinquished his post as Governor and returned to England, ostensibly to attend to family affairs following the death of a kinsman. Soon after his arrival the Crown started prosecution proceedings against him, but – as Charles had perhaps calculated would happen – after a short time the Treasury refused to provide any further funds to pay for commissions to Jamaica and South Carolina to examine witnesses, and the prosecution lapsed. But in 1723 the Marquis reopened the case, and although Charles continued to argue and procrastinate, admitting only to a value of

72

£3,000 for the stolen goods, the case was 'determined by agreement' at the end of 1727 – presumably implying that Charles had to refund at least some of the value of the Marquis's effects.

In the following spring Charles's friends, the Lords Proprietor of Carolina, gave him £1,000 'in consideration of his good services as Governor of South Carolina in defending the Province and repulsing the Indians'; but after this hardly anything else is known about his life in England. In 1735–6, when the official boundary between North and South Carolina was under discussion, he was summoned to London to tell the Government what he remembered on the subject from his sojourn there twenty years earlier. This seems to be the last reference to him in public life until the *Gentleman's Magazine* reported his death: '27.12.1754. Hon. Charles Craven, Esqr., uncle to [4th] Lord Craven, governor of South Carolina in Queen Anne's reign, since which he has lived retired.' This 'retirement' may mean that the court case had reduced him to poverty and social disgrace, or possibly that he had become mentally or physically incapacitated. It would seem that the answer to Caroline's query as to why the Governor did not take more care of his daughters is that he was by then either dead or incapable of so doing.

The widowed Mrs Craven married Mr Jemmett Raymond of Barton Court, Kintbury, in October 1755, less than a year after Mr Craven's death. Once mistress of Barton Court, she was presumably instrumental in arranging her daughter Jane's marriage to the vicar of Kintbury, Revd Thomas Fowle, and also for her son John to marry her second husband's much younger slow-witted half-sister Elizabeth Raymond. Mrs Craven-Raymond died in 1773, and a memorial in Kintbury church bears the busts of herself and her second husband.

11 The elder branch of the Lloyd family had an estate at Pentney, in Norfolk, which had been brought to them by marriage with a Nowys heiress. Caroline's grandfather Nowys was the fourth son of the Revd John Lloyd, vicar of Epping 1710–53, and his wife Isabella. Nowys was born in 1719, and was rector of Bishopston from 1751 until his death in 1789, as well as being rector of Enborne from 1771 onwards. He married Martha Craven in 1763, and their four children were Martha (1765–1843), Eliza (1768–1839), Charles (1769–75) and Mary (1771–1843). The whining toddler jealous of her

sick brother must therefore have been Mary, Caroline's mother.

12   For Mrs Montagu, Mrs Carter and Mrs Vesey, see the *Dictionary of National Biography*.

13   Eliza Lloyd had married her first cousin Fulwar Craven Fowle (1764–1840), who had succeeded his father as vicar of Kintbury and was also rector of Elkstone, Glos. They had six children, all rather older than Caroline.

14   Following Revd Nowys Lloyd's death in 1789, Mrs Lloyd and her two single daughters left Enborne to become tenants of the Revd George Austen at Deane parsonage, where Martha and Mary became close friends of Jane and Cassandra Austen.

      James Austen brought his first wife Anne Mathew home to Deane in 1792, and the Lloyds moved to Ibthorpe. When Mary married James in 1797 Deane parsonage once again became her home until 1801.

15   Until 1865 any cleric entering upon a particular office had to take the following oath:

> I N.N. do swear that I have made no simonaical payment, contract or promise, directly or indirectly, by myself or by any other to my knowledge or with my consent, to any person or persons whatsoever, for or concerning the procuring and obtaining of this ecclesiastical dignity, place, preferment, office or living [here the place is mentioned by name] nor will at any time hereafter perform or satisfy any such kind of payment, contract or promise made by any other without my knowledge or consent. So help me God through Jesus Christ.

(This reference, from Phillimores' *Ecclesiastical Law of the Church of England* (1895), is kindly provided by the Revd W.A.W. Jarvis.)

16   Mrs George Austen (*née* Cassandra Leigh) was a distant cousin of Edward, 5th Lord Leigh of Stoneleigh Abbey, Warwicks. He had died unmarried in 1786, leaving his estate to his unmarried sister, Hon Mary Leigh, for her lifetime. At her death in 1806 the ambiguity of his Will meant there were three claimants to his estate: Mrs Austen's brother Mr James Leigh-Perrot, her first cousin Revd Thomas Leigh, rector of Adlestrop, Glos., and Thomas Leigh's nephew James-Henry Leigh. Revd Thomas Leigh went to Stoneleigh and took

possession in August 1806; Mr Leigh-Perrot settled for a payment of £20,000 down and a £2,000 annuity to himself, and to his wife after his death; and as both these elderly men were childless it was further agreed that the estate should eventually go to the younger James-Henry Leigh, from whom the present Lord Leigh of Stoneleigh is descended.

17   John Bond was the bailiff for the Steventon rectory glebe lands, and is mentioned several times in Jane Austen's letters as coming to talk over farming business with her father.

18   Caroline forgets that in fact Jane Austen was also in the party visiting Godmersham in the summer of 1808. Jane's letters Nos. 51-54 describe the journey and visit, and confirm that the shy little three-year-old Caroline was overwhelmed by her boisterous Kentish cousins.

19   Caroline also forgets, or perhaps never knew, that Edward and George went back to school at Winchester via Southampton, and stayed there with Mrs Austen and their aunts Jane and Cassandra for several days – see Jane's letters Nos. 57, 58 and 59.

20   The baby was Francis William junior, born at Alton on 12 July 1809. Jane wrote her letter No. 68, in verse, to congratulate her brother Frank upon the birth of his first son.

21   Stoneleigh Abbey is indeed a very large house; the West Wing at that date contained twenty-six bedrooms and there were more in the older parts of the house. A central passage stretches the length of the West Wing and has three staircases leading off it – hence Miss Elizabeth Leigh's confusion. The Picture Gallery and double flight of external stone steps were demolished in 1836 and the present North Front built in their place. Mrs Austen and her daughters had gone there in 1806 with the Revd Thomas Leigh, and upon that occasion Mrs Austen wrote a vivid description of the house to Caroline's mother.

Lady Saye and Sele, and Lady Hawke, were yet more of the Leigh cousinhood.

22   Edward Austen had been adopted in his teens by his father's distant childless cousins, Mr and Mrs Thomas Knight of Godmersham Park, Kent, who also owned Chawton Great House. Mr Knight died in 1794, and Edward and his growing family moved to Godmersham in 1797 and old Mrs Knight to Canterbury. When she died in 1812 Edward changed his name to Knight and also took over Chawton Great House as a summer holiday home for himself and family. Miss Deedes

and Miss Cage were two of his nieces by marriage, children of his wife's sisters.

23 Mrs George Austen disapproved of her daughter-in-law's picture, and wrote to her on 14th June 1811: 'Thank you for the sight of your Picture, tho' I can not say it has afforded me pleasure; the upper part of the Face is, I think, like you, so is the Mouth, but the *Nose,* the feature that always most strikes me, is so *unlike* that it spoils the whole; and moreover he has made you look very sour & Cross.'

24 Captain Charles Austen had married Fanny Palmer in Bermuda in 1807 during his naval service in the West Indies, and their first two daughters, Cassandra Esten (1808) and Harriet Jane (1810), were born there. Following their return to England in 1811 a third girl, Frances, was born in 1812, and a fourth, Elizabeth, in 1814. On this occasion, as Caroline relates, both mother and baby died. Charles subsequently married Fanny Palmer's elder sister Harriet in 1820, and by her had another four children.

25 Mr Harwood had hoped to marry the widowed Mrs Heathcote (*née* Elizabeth Bigg, 1773–1855), whose husband Revd William Heathcote had died in 1802. Her one son, William (1801–81), succeeded his uncle as 5th Baronet. Mrs Heathcote was a close friend of Jane Austen and her name occurs frequently in Jane's letters. In letter No. 78 Jane hopes her friend will marry Mr Harwood, and in No. 78.1 she refers specifically to the poverty of the Harwood family.

26 Mr Lovelace Bigg-Wither (1741–1813) of Manydown House. His daughters Elizabeth (Mrs Heathcote), Catherine (Mrs Hill) and Alethea were old friends of Jane Austen, and his son Harris (1781–1833) proposed marriage to her. The family are frequently mentioned in Jane's letters.

27 Henry Austen's first wife was his cousin Eliza (1761–1813), daughter of the Revd George Austen's sister Philadelphia. Eliza had lived in France and married first, the Comte de Feuillide, who was guillotined in 1794. In 1796 Caroline's father James had tried to marry her, but she had rejected him in favour of his younger brother Henry. It was after this disappointment that James married Mary Lloyd, who had never been on good terms with Eliza in consequence.

28 The Vine (nowadays spelt 'Vyne' and owned by the National Trust) is a large house in the parish of Sherborne St John, and was then in the possession of the Chute family. At the time of which Caroline writes the owners were Mr and Mrs William

John Chute. They were childless, so had adopted as their daughter Caroline Wiggett, a distant cousin of Mr Chute. James Austen was vicar of Sherborne St John, and so usually dined with the Chutes at The Vine after doing Sunday duty at the church, quite often taking James-Edward with him.

Mr Chute's sister Mary was the wife of Mr Wither Bramston of nearby Oakley Hall. The Beach family of Netheravon were also connected with the Chutes by marriage.

29 'Miss Smith' was Mrs Chute's unmarried sister; in later years she and Mrs Chute became the aunts-in-law of James-Edward.

30 The Chawton estate had been owned early in the eighteenth century by a Mrs Elizabeth Knight. She left it to a kinsman Thomas Brodnax May, who changed his name to Knight and later built Godmersham Park in Kent. It was his son, Thomas Knight II, who adopted Edward Austen; on the maternal side, Thomas Knight II's great-grandmother had been a Jane Austen of an earlier generation, so that he was therefore a distant cousin of the Steventon Austens. The lawsuit arose because Thomas Knight II was the last member of the Brodnax family, to whom the Chawton estate was entailed; failing them, other distant cousins of the old Mrs. Elizabeth Knight could have a claim. It was these heirs-at-law whom Edward Austen had to pay off so expensively.

31 Anna Austen, aged 21, married Benjamin Lefroy, the youngest son of Jane Austen's old friend Madam Lefroy of Ashe. Ben's elder brother John Henry George had become rector of Ashe following their father's death.

32 Mr William Digweed was the tenant of Steventon Manor House, and nearest neighbour to the Austens at Steventon rectory.

33 The Deane parish registers show that Thomas Whitehead Dennis, son of Thomas and Elizabeth Dennis, was baptised on 23 February 1815, the day of his father's funeral.

34 The Debary family consisted of the Revd Peter (1764–1841), vicar of Eversley from 1807 onwards, and his sisters Ann, Mary, Susannah and Sarah. Mary Lloyd had known the family since her Hurstbourne Tarrant days, as their father had been vicar of that parish, and she had asked the eldest sister to stay with her at Deane to help when James-Edward was born in 1798. They are mentioned occasionally in Jane Austen's letters, but she did not much care for them.

35 Henry Austen's illness is described in Jane's letters Nos. 111, 116, 117 and 118.

36 Captain Austen's ship *Phoenix* was wrecked during a hurricane off the coast of Asia Minor, near Smyrna.

37 Caroline was wrong in thinking that her Uncle Henry had left Oxford without graduating; he was made BA in 1792 and MA in 1796, but because of the Napoleonic war had decided to go into the militia rather than the church. Later on he became an army agent and then a banker. After ordination his first appointment was as curate of Chawton, though Caroline makes a mistake in her manuscript and writes 'Alton' instead.

38 It was in 1816 that Jane Austen first began to feel the onset of her fatal illness, and the trip to Cheltenham was undertaken in the hope of being cured by the spa waters.

39 'Founder's Kin' was an Oxford University custom, originating in the thirteenth century, whereby young men descended either directly or collaterally from founders of colleges could have preferential treatment, when applying for scholarships at the University, over those not so descended. The custom was finally abolished in the middle of the last century.

James-Edward could have applied for a Founder's Kin scholarship at St John's College, as through his father and Austen grandmother he could trace collateral descent from Sir Thomas White, founder of the College in 1566. However, it seems he preferred to enter Exeter College, and to try for a Craven Scholarship, by virtue of his mother's Craven ancestry.

40 The register of St Egwin's, Norton (now in the Hereford and Worcester County Record Office) shows that six of Charles Craven's children were baptised there between 1725 and 1732.

41 Mr James Leigh-Perrot was the brother of Mrs George Austen, and therefore Caroline's great-uncle. As his uncle was childless, James Austen had expected to become the heir; but Mr Leigh-Perrot left his property to his wife for her lifetime, and only thereafter to James. The widowed Mrs Leigh-Perrot outlived James, so he never derived any benefit from his uncle's Will.

42 Details of Caroline's memories of her aunt Jane are given separately in *My Aunt Jane Austen* (1952).

43 Revd William Gilpin, vicar of Boldre in the New Forest, was well-known for his books describing the artistic or 'pictures-

que' aspects of landscape scenery. The book James had in mind here was *Observations on the River Wye and several parts of South Wales, etc., Relative Chiefly to Picturesque Beauty* (1782).

44 Jane Austen's close friend Catherine Bigg had married in 1808 the Revd Herbert Hill, rector of Streatham. He was an uncle of Robert Southey, the Poet Laureate, and of Robert's younger brother Dr Henry Herbert Southey, who had a practice in Queen Anne Street, London.

45 Caroline could not remember the number of the house in Great Russell Street in which they lodged, but their friend Mrs Chute of The Vine noted it down as being No. 107. The house still exists, now re-numbered 99, and retains the black and white marble chequered floor to the entrance hall, handsome wide staircase and painted ceiling depicting Bacchus and Ariadne. The drawing-rooms at the rear look northwards towards Hampstead, though the garden has now more or less been built over.

46 Scarlets, at Hare Hatch, Berks, was the house that Mr Leigh-Perrot had bought at the time of his marriage in 1764. After his death in 1817 his widow lived there until 1836 and then bequeathed it to James-Edward; within a few years he found it too expensive to keep up, so in 1853 he first leased and then in 1863 sold it.

47 Henry Austen's second marriage was on 11 April 1820 (not March, as Caroline wrote) to Miss Eleanor Jackson, a niece of the rector of Chawton.

48 Miss Murden was an aged relation of the Fowles, and had at one time lived in Southampton while Mrs Austen and her her daughters were also there. She is mentioned in several of Jane's letters.

49 Not only was Mrs Austen's brother Thomas Leigh mentally handicapped, but her second son George (1766–1838) had also been abnormal since early childhood. He too lived with his uncle under the care of the Culham family at Monk Sherborne.

50 During his boyhood visits to The Vine, James-Edward had met Mrs Chute's widowed sister Mrs Augusta Smith and her family of six daughters and three sons. It was the second of these daughters, Emma (1801–1876) whom he now married.

51 The Mrs F. Austen mentioned here is Captain Frank Austen's second wife, Caroline's maternal aunt Martha Lloyd, whom he had only recently married following the death of his first

wife in childbirth in 1823.

52 James-Edward's family grew to be: Cholmeley (1829–99), Emma Cassandra (Amy) (1831–1902), Charles Edward (1832–1924), Spencer (1834–1913), Arthur Henry (1836–1917), Mary Augusta (1838–1922), Edward Compton (1839–1916), Augustus (1840–1926), George Raymond (1841–2), William (1843–1921).

53 At Ben Lefroy's early death Anna was left with seven children: Anna Jemima (1815–55), Julia Cassandra (1816–84), George Benjamin Austen (1818–1910), Fanny Caroline (1820–85), Georgiana Brydges (1822–82), Louisa Langlois (1824–1910), Elizabeth Lucy (1827–96).

54 Caroline writes her description of the Kintbury riots from memory long after the event, but her brother and his wife were at Newtown at the time, so that Emma was able to write an eye-witness account to her aunt Mrs Chute at The Vine:

> That day [Tuesday 23rd November 1830] we came here from Sulham by the Newbury road & as we came near to Newbury a man on horseback told us that two *thousand* of the mob were going to enter the town & that he had *seen* them. This intelligence frightened me very much but Edward doubted the truth of it & we soon found it was a false alarm. Newbury was however in a state of great excitement & I fancy a mob was expected – but at Ld Cravens it turned back to Kintbury the place of its origin.
>
> At Newtown we found them expecting *another* mob – partly Burghclere people. They went to Mr. Villebois & broke his threshing machine, drift plough, &c, & then to Sir James Fellowes & broke his machine after that they came nearer to us & we heard the sound of a great many voices in a joyous tone & of some melancholy cow horns.
>
> Mr Arbuthnot has no machines & he met the people at the brook where there is an alehouse. He desired them not to come up to him but like the other gentlemen considered himself obliged to give them money. They demanded it upon which he said he wd. not comply with a *demand* but he would *give* it them to refresh themselves with & advised them to go home quietly. In short he felt he could not help it. They staid refreshing themselves at the alehouse but do not seem to have been riotous – paid for what they had & then went away. The landlord of the house told us

that he did not hear a word *awry*. I was most thankful that they did not come up here. The next day Wednesday the gentlemen rode about in search of them for now they felt strong; both Lancers & Grenadier Guards having arrived in Newbury & on this day between 90 & 100 rioters were made prisoners. Yesterday they were under examination at Newbury in two courts one for Berkshire (where Mr Dundas presides) the other for Hants - magistrates Sir James Fellowes & Mr Mount. It seems that against some there is accusation enough to hang them for extorting money & even doing so from passengers on the high road. I hope however that a great many of the 100 will be dismissed. Now I should hope that our part of the country is quiet; this examination is to go on to-day. The Newbury constables & gentlemen have been well disposed to exert themselves & on Tuesday went out a strong party to Ld. Cravens but found they could not act then, as a promise had been given that if the mob would go home quietly they should not be molested.

55 In her Will Mrs Leigh-Perrot left legacies to her own maternal relatives (the Cholmeleys, Welbys and Glascotts), with the residue to James-Edward Austen provided he took the name of Leigh. She also left him the Scarlets estate, and £1,000 apiece to his sisters Anna and Caroline. Admiral Francis Austen received £6,000, Captain Charles £4,000, Cassandra £5,000, Edward Knight £2,000, and Henry only £1,000, as Mrs Leigh-Perrot had not forgiven him for losing family money when his banking business failed. Her faithful servant Hannah also received £2,000.

56 The Portsmouth Floating Bridge was incorporated in 1838 and opened in 1840 to provide a direct link from Portsmouth Point to Gosport. It was a flat-bottomed almost raft-like boat, large enough to take horses and carriages as well as cabin passengers. The boat was attached to chains, and pulled to and fro across the harbour by steam power. Its capital was £16,000 in £25 shares, £11,000 in £12 10s shares, and £9,000 by mortgage. However, business fluctuated considerably over the years, and Caroline made a loss when she sold her shares. The last of the Bridge's three vessels continued in use until 1959.

57 Apart from these last few remaining childish verses, Caroline's stories are referred to in several of her aunt Jane's letters.